PEOPLE

IN THE NEWS

Stephen King

by John F. Wukovits

Lucent Books, San Diego, CA

Titles in the People in the News series include:

Jim Carrey
Bill Gates
John Grisham
Michael Jordan
Dominique Moceanu

Rosie O'Donnell
The Rolling Stones
Steven Spielberg
Oprah Winfrey
Tiger Woods

To My Daughter Amy
You Make Me Smile

Library of Congress Cataloging-in-Publication Data

Wukovits, John F., 1944–
   Stephen King / by John F. Wukovits.
      p. cm. — (People in the news)
   Includes bibliographical references (p.   ) and index.
   Summary: Discusses the life, career, and influence of the popular horror writer Stephen King.
   ISBN 1-56006-562-1 (lib. bdg. : alk. paper)
   1. King, Stephen, 1947–   Juvenile literature. 2. Horror tales, American—History and criticism—Juvenile literature. 3. Novelists, American—20th century—Biography—Juvenile literature. [1. King, Stephen, 1947–   . 2. Authors, American.] I. Title. II. Series: People in the news (San Diego, Calif.)
PS3561.I483Z96   1999
813'.54—dc21
[B]   99-20085
                                                                      CIP

Copyright © 1999 by Lucent Books, Inc.
P.O. Box 289011
San Diego, CA 92198-9011
Printed in the U.S.A.

Table of Contents

Foreword

FAME AND CELEBRITY are alluring. People are drawn to those who walk in fame's spotlight, whether they are known for great accomplishments or for notorious deeds. The lives of the famous pique public interest and attract attention, perhaps because their experiences seem in some ways so different from, yet in other ways so similar to, our own.

Newspapers, magazines, and television regularly capitalize on this fascination with celebrity by running profiles of famous people. For example, television programs such as *Entertainment Tonight* devote all of their programming to stories about entertainment and entertainers. Magazines such as *People* fill their pages with stories of the private lives of famous people. Even newspapers, newsmagazines, and television news frequently delve into the lives of well-known personalities. Despite the number of articles and programs, few provide more than a superficial glimpse at their subjects.

Lucent's People in the News series offers young readers a deeper look into the lives of today's newsmakers, the influences that have shaped them, and the impact they have had in their fields of endeavor and on other people's lives. The subjects of the series hail from many disciplines and walks of life. They include authors, musicians, athletes, political leaders, entertainers, entrepreneurs, and others who have made a mark on modern life and who, in many cases, will continue to do so for years to come.

These biographies are more than factual chronicles. Each book emphasizes the contributions, accomplishments, or deeds that have brought fame or notoriety to the individual and shows how that person has influenced modern life. Authors portray their subjects in a realistic, unsentimental light. For example, Bill Gates—the cofounder and chief executive officer of the software giant Microsoft—has been instrumental in making personal computers the most vital tool of the modern age. Few dispute his business savvy, his perseverance, or his technical expertise, yet critics say he is ruthless in his dealings with competitors and driven more by his desire to maintain Microsoft's dominance in the computer industry than by an interest in furthering technology.

In these books, young readers will encounter inspiring stories about real people who achieved success despite enormous obstacles. Oprah Winfrey—the most powerful, most watched, and wealthiest woman on television today—spent the first six years of her life in the care of her grandparents while her unwed mother sought work and a better life elsewhere. Her adolescence was colored by promiscuity, pregnancy at age fourteen, rape, and sexual abuse.

Each author documents and supports his or her work with an array of primary and secondary source quotations taken from diaries, letters, speeches, and interviews. All quotes are footnoted to show readers exactly how and where biographers derive their information and provide guidance for further research. The quotations enliven the text by giving readers eyewitness views of the life and accomplishments of each person covered in the People in the News series.

In addition, each book in the series includes photographs, annotated bibliographies, timelines, and comprehensive indexes. For both the casual reader and the student researcher, the People in the News series offers insight into the lives of today's newsmakers—people who shape the way we live, work, and play in the modern age.

Introduction

"His Genius Is to Make Horror Acceptable"

ALMOST SINGLE-HANDEDLY Stephen King has transformed horror writing into a popular literary genre. Though numerous other authors, such as Edgar Allan Poe, Mary Shelley, and H. P. Lovecraft paved the path before him, none had the impact that King has had on the public. Readers who had previously ignored that genre became interested in King's many novels. His popularity so exploded that fans eagerly awaited the arrival of each new book. Some of his titles remained on the paperback best-seller list for over ten years; at one point, five King books simultaneously appeared on the *New York Times* best-seller list, an achievement unrivalled by any other author.

Before Stephen King appeared on the scene, horror books occupied a status inferior to what critics considered "serious" fiction and

Stephen King is often credited with turning the genre of horror into a respectable literary style.

nonfiction. King changed that. As fellow horror writer Clive Barker states, "I think his genius is to make horror acceptable, to make it acceptable to read on the train without covering it behind the cover of the new John Updike novel."[1] Barker added that King "has turned the horror genre—so long an underdog on the publishing scene—into a force to be reckoned with."[2]

Rather than viewing King's work with disdain, as they did earlier in his career, a growing number of university professors now seriously examine King's writing. Academic conferences produce papers on King's impact on popular culture, and fellow writers look to his work as a standard by which they measure their own material.

King's Success

King succeeds because he forces readers to face their own worst fears, just as King confronts those fears when he writes. Death, funerals, rats, and insects—all items that scare King—inhabit his novels. He unites those fears with the familiar and ordinary—a small town, often set in Maine; a teenage girl; a car—and crafts a riveting tale that grabs the reader from the first page and refuses to let go. In his only nonfiction book, *Danse Macabre*, King writes, "We make up horrors to help us cope with the real ones. The dream of horror is in itself an outletting and a lancing . . . and it may well be that the mass-media dream of horror can sometimes become a nationwide analyst's couch." King claims that readers swarm to horror because it contains the "ability to form a liaison between our fantasy fears and our real fears."[3]

In a magazine interview, King explains the three different ways in which he attempts to scare the reader: "Naturally, I'll try to terrify you first, and if that doesn't work, I'll try to horrify you, and if I can't make it there, I'll try to gross you out."[4] When his readers finish one of his novels, King wants them to be afraid to peer over their shoulders or hesitant to take their first step toward the basement.

King believes that people love to be frightened. As he told the *Chicago Tribune*,

> There are some people whose lives are full of fears—that their marriage isn't working, that they aren't going to

make it on the job, that society is crumbling all around them. But we're not really supposed to talk about things like that, and so they don't have any outlets for all those scary feelings. But the horror writer can give them a place to put their fears, and it's OK to be afraid then, because nothing is real, and you can blow it all away when it's over.[5]

Another reason King succeeds is because he writes about people with whom he is familiar, and he places those individuals in unusual circumstances. King says that "the stories themselves may be unbelievable. But within the framework of the stories I'm concerned that what people do in these stories should be as real as possible and that the characters of the people should be as real as possible."[6]

A Publishing Phenomenon

King has succeeded in a variety of formats, including books, movies, and television. His novels, from *Carrie* in 1974 to his most recent offerings, have sold millions of copies. Because of his books' popularity, filmmakers have also adapted them for movies. His books, including *The Stand* and *The Langoliers*, have also been made into television miniseries.

King's amazing string of best-sellers has made him one of the wealthiest writers in the world, earning $25 million in 1995–1996. One contract he signed with a major publishing company garnered $30 million for four books. Most recently, King offered his newest novel, *Bag of Bones*, for auction to the publisher who produced the highest bid—with a starting price of $17 million.

Because of King's profound influence on American popular literature, *People* magazine selected him as one of its "Twenty Who Defined the Decade" of the 1980s. When *Publishers Weekly* compiled its list of the top twenty-five best-selling fiction books of the decade, seven belonged to King, including *The Tommyknockers* at number three, *It* at number ten, and *Misery* at number fifteen.

King has enjoyed a remarkable quarter-century of publishing success because he refuses to settle into a comfortable niche.

Stephen King signs autographs at a Tower Books appearance. King's books have made him one of the most popular authors of the last two decades.

Though a handful of common themes wind through many of his books, King continues to evolve as a writer and tries to explore new themes. As Sharon Russell writes in her critical study of the author, *Stephen King: A Critical Companion,*

> One of the most notable aspects of King's development as a writer has been his ability to continue to grow. He has not let fame force him into repeating patterns which are proven successes. He has never been afraid to go against critical opinion. He knows that many critics dismiss him because they do not know how to deal seriously with authors who write popular fiction. He does not write to please his critics.[7]

The Critics

Despite King's accomplishments, reviewers often attack his writing style. When *The Shining* appeared in 1977, the *New York Times Book Review* concluded, "To say that Stephen King is not an elegant writer is putting it mildly." Another reviewer bluntly declared that King was "a writer of fairly engaging and preposterous claptrap."[8]

Other critics relegate horror fiction to the backwaters of literature and refuse to accept the idea that it belongs with "legitimate" writing. One question that has hounded King throughout his career is "When are you going to write something serious?" "My answer," King responds, "is that I'm as serious as I can be every time I sit down at a typewriter."[9]

King tries to shrug off the criticism and take solace in the fact that he has reached millions of readers throughout the world. His works have been translated into thirty-two different languages, making his name and visage recognizable on every inhabited continent. *Time* magazine heralded his prominence as the nation's leading writer of horror by placing King on the cover of its October 6, 1985, issue.

Few authors have attained the degree of success enjoyed by Stephen King. Financially secure, King can set his own schedule, live anywhere, and indulge his and his family's wishes. However, the path to security did not unfold easily for King, who experienced a difficult childhood and school career and then struggled to make ends meet in his early years as a professional writer.

Chapter 1

"If It Was Junk, It Was *Magic* Junk"

As HE DOES in the books he writes, Stephen Edwin King shocked people even before his birth on September 21, 1947, at Maine General Hospital in Portland, Maine. Two years before Stephen's birth, physicians had informed his father, Donald Edward King, and his mother, Nellie Ruth Pillsbury King, that they would never be able to conceive children. In 1945 they adopted a son, David Victor King. To their great surprise, less than two years later Nellie became pregnant.

Nellie King boasted a Scottish lineage and claimed that she was related to the renowned Pillsbury family of baked-goods fame. Stephen King later wrote, "The difference between the two branches, Mom said, was that the flour-Pillsburys moved west to make their fortune, while our people stayed shirttail but honest on the coast of Maine." [10]

King's father, whose family immigrated to Indiana from Ireland, could not long remain in one spot. King wrote years later that his father "was a man with an itchy foot." [11] After serving in the merchant marine in World War II, Donald married Nellie, but the responsibilities of a family proved to be more of a burden than he could handle. When Stephen was only two years old, his father deserted the family and has never been seen since.

Absentee Parent

"I don't remember him at all," [12] King later wrote of his father. When Stephen was about eleven years old, he and his brother discovered a movie reel that was filmed by their father while he was aboard ship during World War II. Though they had little money between them, the excited youngsters pooled their resources to rent a movie projector, then sat down with anticipation to get their first glimpse of their missing father.

King writes that they impatiently waited as footage of life on a merchant marine vessel unfolded, but since their father was the cameraman, no shots of him appeared. Suddenly the boys spotted Donald King. According to Stephen King, he and his brother

> watched it over and over again in fascinated silence. My father turned the camera over to someone else at one point and there he is, Donald King of Peru, Indiana, standing against the rail. He raises his hand; smiles; unknowingly waves to sons who were then not even conceived. We rewound it, watched it, rewound it, watched it again. And again.

Writing in *Danse Macabre*, King adds a rebuke for his absent parent: "Hi, Dad; wonder where you are now." [13]

In 1964 King's mother was positive she had spotted her husband on a television report about a group of white mercenary soldiers fighting in Africa. Though Stephen King agreed that it might be possible, neither he nor his brother took any action to locate the man. Years later, when a news reporter asked King if his father was still alive, the author replied, "I have no clue. . . . For all intents and purposes, he just vanished." [14]

Frequent Moves

With no one to support the practically penniless family, Nellie packed her meager belongings and, with her two children, commenced a nine-year series of moves around the eastern and midwestern United States. "We hopscotched our way across the country during those nine years," [15] said Stephen King. Always staying with relatives on his mother's side, the trio lived at various times in five towns: Malden, Massachusetts; Stratford, Connecticut; Chicago, Illinois; West De Pere, Wisconsin; and Fort Wayne, Indiana.

A Nightmare to Recall

When King was five or six years old, he experienced a particularly frightening nightmare that he has never forgotten. He explains the dream in his autobiography, *Danse Macabre*.

> In this dream I saw the body of a hanged man dangling from the arm of a scaffold on a hill. Rooks perched on the shoulders of the corpse, and behind it was a noxious green sky, boiling with clouds. This corpse bore a sign: ROBERT BURNS. But when the wind caused the corpse to turn in the air, I saw that it was my face—rotted and picked by the birds, but obviously mine. And then the corpse opened its eyes and looked at me. I woke up screaming, sure that that dead face would be leaning over me in the dark.

While he does not believe that dreams or any childhood incident, no matter how gruesome, tranformed him into a horror writer, he has frequently used content of his dreams and memories in his novels. He included the nightmare in *'Salem's Lot*, for example, and in later books other familiar people, places, and events appear.

The moves placed enormous strains on Stephen King, who not only had to live without a father but also had to adjust to different families and unfamiliar people with each successive move. He found it hard to make friends, for he never knew how long he might remain. As King later explained, "I often felt unhappy and different, estranged from other kids my age." [16] In 1958, when Stephen was eleven years old, the three returned to Maine and settled in the small town of Durham, where Nellie could take care of her ailing parents.

One of Stephen King's friends described Durham as "a working-class town—in a sense, a hard-luck town." [17] Fewer than one thousand people inhabited the area and most squeezed out a living by working in factories or on small farms.

Life in Durham

The Kings experienced worse living conditions than their neighbors did. Their two-story house contained no indoor plumbing—an outhouse in the backyard provided that basic necessity. They fetched water from a nearby well, unless it ran dry, in which case Stephen and David would have to walk to a nearby spring and haul the water home in buckets. When the boys or their mother wanted a hot bath or shower, they had to walk a half mile down the road to their aunt's home.

To keep one step ahead of the bill collector, Nellie labored long hours at an assortment of jobs. As a result, the boys did not see much of their mother. Stephen King praises his mother for keeping the family together and providing for them as well as she could. He recalls that "she kept things together. . . . We never had a car (nor a TV set until 1956), but we never missed any meals." [18] However, he adds, "We didn't have desserts when I grew up." [19]

Love of Reading and Horror

Nellie King's influence on Stephen is undeniable. Although she lacked formal education, Nellie pushed her sons to excel in school and to establish goals for the future. King remembers that his mother was

> a very hardheaded person when it came to success. She knew what it was like to be on her own without an education, and she was determined that David and I would go to college. "You're not going to punch a time clock all your life," she told us. She always told us that dreams and ambitions can cause bitterness if they're not realized, and she encouraged me to submit my writings. [20]

Nellie King may have performed her greatest service to Stephen by imparting to him a love of reading. Though she worked fifty hours each week, she always made time for her stack of books, which she called "a pile of cheap, sweet vacations." [21] If Stephen asked her to read to him, she would put aside her choice of the day—usually a mystery story—and open an illustrated version of *Treasure Island* or some other well-regarded book.

When Stephen was seven years old, he once asked his mother what book she was reading. "Oh, you wouldn't like this one," she replied. "This one's a really scary one. It's about a man who changes into someone else. It's called *Dr. Jekyll and Mr. Hyde.*" When her son persisted, she feebly attempted to dissuade him, then happily gave in, "because she loved that stuff [reading horror]; she absolutely adored it. If there was anything she loved better than that, it was passing the scare on to somebody else." [22]

The two sat on the porch each evening that summer, and Stephen listened as his mother read *Dr. Jekyll and Mr. Hyde*, by Robert Louis Stevenson. "That was a happy summer for me," he recalled.

> I lived and died with that story, with Mr. Utterson and with poor Dr. Jekyll, and particularly with Dr. Jekyll's other side, which was every vestige of pretense of civilization thrown away. I can remember lying in bed, wakeful after that night's reading was done, and what I usually thought of was how Mr. Hyde walked over the little girl, back and forth, breaking her bones; and it was such a terrible image and I thought, *I have to do that; but I have to do that worse*. [23]

Other Influences

Other factors steered the young King toward writing and horror. When Stephen was four years old, he asked if he could listen to a radio adaptation of science fiction writer Ray Bradbury's "Mars Is Heaven!" His mother refused, saying that the program would be too intense for such a young boy, and told him to go upstairs to his bedroom. "I crept down to the door to listen, anyway," King explained later, "and she was right: it was plenty upsetting." Stephen rushed back upstairs, but "I didn't sleep in my bed that night; that night I slept in the doorway, where the real and rational light of the bathroom bulb could shine on my face." [24]

A steady diet of science fiction and horror magazines and books fueled King's interest in reading. He eagerly read the latest issues of comic books such as *Weird Science, Tales from the Crypt*, and *Tales from the Vault*, as well as books like *Invasion of the Body Snatchers, The Thing*, and *It Came from Outer Space*.

In addition to reading horror stories, King started writing them at an early age. By the time he was old enough to attend school, King had written a handful of tales. "The earliest writing

I can remember doing is when I was stuck in bed with the flu and started copying Tom Swift books into a tablet, changing the stories as I went along." Though these could hardly be called original productions, King found he was hooked on writing. "Once you get a taste of that kind of power, you're lost forever."[25] By age seven he had penned his initial horror story, in which a dinosaur terrorized a small town.

Movies also influenced King. The next best thing to reading a horror story was viewing one, so Stephen and

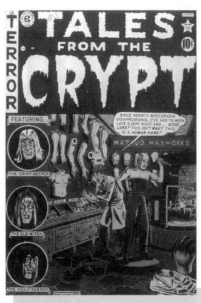

One of King's biggest influences came from Tales from the Crypt, *a comic book he read as a child.*

David rarely missed an opportunity to rush to the nearest theater whenever a horror movie arrived. Stephen would respond to the movies he saw by rewriting the plots. After watching *The Pit and the Pendulum,* for instance, King hurried home and wrote his own version.

The film that influenced him the most was the classic 1950s horror movie *Creature from the Black Lagoon.* According to King, it was the "first movie I can remember seeing as a kid." He explains the movie's impact: "I knew, watching, that the Creature had become *my* Creature; . . . just as I knew that, later on that night, he would visit me in the black lagoon of my dreams, looking much more realistic."[26] Stephen left the theater exclaiming to his mother, "I wanna do that! I'm really scared. I want to make people as scared as I am."[27]

School

Although King received enormous satisfaction from watching movies and reading books, school was another matter. Tall for his age, overweight, disheveled in appearance, and wearing black thick-rimmed glasses, King did not look like someone destined to succeed. Many of the other kids in the sparsely furnished one-room Durham schoolhouse either avoided or teased him. When classmates lined up to pick teams for a quick game of baseball or football, King was usually the last one selected because, as he explains, "I was fat and wore glasses."[28] The team that had to take King heard derisive laughs from the other squad and remarks such as "Ha-ha, you got King."[29]

As one friend, Brian Hall, recalls, "Steve was a big, klutzy kid . . . . Uncoordinated. Walking down the road you knew he was going to fall down or walk into a sign, reading his book."[30]

King brushed off the taunts by reminding himself of the talents he possessed. "I could write, and that was the way I defined myself, even as a kid."[31] King's teacher noticed that he always seemed to be writing a story or play, usually about outer space or a hideous monster. When she graded his papers, the writing in them easily surpassed that of the other students. At graduation

Another major influence on King was the classic 1950s horror film Creature from the Black Lagoon.

from the one-room schoolhouse in 1962, King owned the dubious distinction of being named the top student—of a three-student class!

Christopher Chesley

When King was twelve, he met Christopher Chesley, a younger student who lived one-half mile away. As King walked into the Durham school, Chesley recalled thinking that King "looked like a kid with those old-fashioned, black-rimmed glasses. His hair was kind of messy and he was kind of slow. He was chunky, but not fat."[32] From the start, the two became fast friends.

One day after school King invited Chesley to his home. When Chesley entered King's bedroom and saw the books and old typewriter, he coaxed a reluctant King to show him some of the stories he had written. Chesley read through a few stories and liked what he read. "To go inside his house was like being pulled into a different world unlike old, unimaginative Durham with its cowsheds."[33]

King and Chesley were practically inseparable in those years. They frequently talked about writing and books, and they periodically hitchhiked into the town of Lewiston to watch horror movies at its theater. One time they heard about a serious boating accident in nearby Runaround Pond. Like most teenage boys, the curious pair hurried over to investigate. "When we got to Runaround Pond," recalls Chesley, "they had dragged the body up, with lights shining on it. They had not covered up the corpse yet."[34] This first sight of a dead body rattled the two teenagers, and King later wrote this incident into one of his short stories.

King shared his hopes and dreams with Chesley, who also loved writing. When King was fourteen, he told Chesley that he would be a success: "You know what I'm gonna do the first time I hit it big, Chris? You know what I'm gonna do? I'm gonna get myself a great big Cadillac!" Chesley later admitted, "I always wanted that for him because I knew how badly he wanted it."[35]

Lovecraft and Horror

A major event that forever linked King's name with the horror genre occurred on a cold fall day in 1959 or 1960. Over the garage of King's aunt's home was a storage room where family members deposited old clothes and other unneeded items. King described it as "a kind of family museum," and that day he decided to investigate the room's contents. In one section, King recalls, "I happened to come on a box of my father's books . . . paperbacks from the mid-forties."[36] One by one King pulled out each volume and stared in awe at the covers. Cemeteries at night, monsters lurking from behind tombstones, and other images leaped off the covers and into his mind.

What King had uncovered was a collection of stories by H. P. Lovecraft, an early twentieth-century American writer of horror books. Lovecraft was one of the first serious writers of horror in this century, and his work influenced other talented authors, including Ray Bradbury, Jack Finney, and Richard Matheson.

King found in Lovecraft a model for his own style. He admired how Lovecraft removed horror from its usual European settings and placed it in New England. As Christopher Chesley

The work of science fiction writer Ray Bradbury influenced the young Stephen King.

explains, "What Steve learned from Lovecraft was the possibility of taking the New England atmosphere and using that as a spring-board. . . . *Dracula* could be moved to Durham, basically." [37] After that encounter with Lovecraft's work, King and horror became inextricably linked. "I was on my way," remembers King. "Lovecraft—courtesy of my father—opened the way for me." [38]

King Starts to Write

King would retreat to the cramped bedroom he shared with his brother to create his stories. Sitting amidst his books—"We didn't have any bookcases, so all our paperbacks lined the walls of the room on the floor" [39]—ghosts, creatures, rats, and insects flowed from King's fertile imagination.

When King was about twelve years old, he crafted a slick version of a screenplay for a horror movie, ran off copies on an ancient duplicating machine, and sold them at school for a dime until the teacher made him stop. About this same time, King also wrote a twenty-page story about a group of students who took over a grammar school but died when the National Guard attacked. He used many of his classmates as characters, and Chesley recalls that "the kids he liked best 'died' last; so naturally, we were all wondering when we were going to 'die.'" [40]

Though he gained popularity among classmates and friends with his early efforts, King did not always receive the approval of teachers and relatives, who considered horror stories to be a waste of time. Furthermore, rather than disappearing into his room to write, some adults believed King should be playing sports like football or attending school functions. As Chesley recounts, "Everybody thought—considering how much he read and how much he wrote—that he spent way too much time in his room, too much time in his imagination, and it was thought to be unhealthy and abnormal behavior." [41]

While King shrugged it off by claiming that "if it was junk, it was *magic* junk," the criticism hurt. Sensitive to the rebukes, King retreated further into his self-imposed isolation. Chesley stated that, because of the criticism, "Steve felt more alone; he felt a sense of isolation." Chesley adds that, "given who he was,

King Appears in *Dave's Rag*

In January 1959 Stephen King's brother, David, produced the first in a series of newsletters named *Dave's Rag*. Written by the two King brothers and delivered to a group of neighbors who signed on as subscribers, the newsletter contained tidbits of local information, news of family gatherings, and assorted movie and television reviews.

Stephen J. Spignesi writes in his *The Complete Stephen King Encyclopedia* that one issue sported an advertisement urging readers to "WATCH FOR THE NEW KING STORY!!!!" The story, called "Land of 1,000,000 Years Ago," received a favorable, if somewhat biased, advanced billing. "Exciting story of 21 people prisoners on an island that should have been extinct 1,000,000 years ago. Order through this newspaper."

In the same issue appeared Stephen King's review of the new fall television shows. The effort illustrates the twelve-year-old Stephen King's deep interest in writing. The desire to write was present, and he would have plenty of time to work on his style. In *The Stephen King Story*, George Beahm relates the young author's conclusion.

> Well, the fall T.V. season is in full swing, and it has the newest and best shows since the beginning of T.V. There's T.V. for every fan. Like adventure or espionage? Try the "Trouble Shooters" or "Five Fingers." Westerns your preference? How about "The Deputy" or "Man from Blackhawk." Westerns are the most numerous this season. Science fiction? Try "Man into Space" or "Twilight Zone." Roughly 20 new fall shows. Happy viewing. Steve King.

though, the isolation was necessary to make him what he became."[42] The ridicule toughened the introspective youth and helped fashion his point of view.

In 1959 King's brother began publishing a newsletter titled *Dave's Rag*, in which he and Stephen reported on any topic that struck their fancy. Movie reviews, television show summaries, and local announcements filled the columns of the little newsletter, which the two boys delivered to their twenty paying subscribers. Some editions even carried ads for books Stephen King had yet to write, suggesting that the young author harbored grand dreams for his future.

King's early school years had deepened his love for writing. High school and college now beckoned, waiting to hand him experiences that would determine his path and teachers who would guide him.

Chapter 2

"This Boy Has Shown Evidence of Some Talent"

Because Durham did not have its own high school, the town arranged for its students to be driven in an old limousine to Lisbon High in nearby Lisbon Falls, Maine. In the fall of 1962 King climbed into the rusty vehicle for his first ride to his new school. At Lisbon High he would produce his initial efforts at serious writing, which would provide personal satisfaction. King's high school years, though, were far from happy.

An Average Student

King's academic effort hardly earned distinction for the shy teenager. Only twice he appeared on the honor roll—once in each of his first two years—but chemistry and other science classes kept him off the remainder of the time. While collecting A's and B's in history and literature courses, King usually could do no better than C's or D's in the sciences.

Though hesitant to join in with most of the students at parties and other school functions, King did participate in some extracurricular activities. With his height advantage, King became the football team's starting offensive left tackle. He also played rhythm guitar in a rock band named the MoonSpinners. Each time he remained after school for football practice or any other reason, however, King had to walk or hitchhike the six miles home since Durham's rented limousine could not wait for him.

King was reserved and found it difficult to relax in large crowds. His circle included a small number of good friends, especially Chesley, although he attended a different high school. After school King shared activities and thoughts with Chesley, who recalls that King did not seem particularly happy in school. "I've always assumed that he didn't have a wonderful high school experience, that it wasn't that great a time for him in his life."[43]

King was never subjected to serious criticism or teasing from classmates, but he would never have won a popularity contest, either. He enjoyed some of his classes and the few extra activities in which he was involved, but after school he preferred to read, write, or lounge around in his bedroom. "I wasn't the kind of kid who would get elected to student council," he explained, "but neither did I lurk around the lockers looking like I was just waiting for somebody to haul off on me."[44]

King's taste in literature broadened during his high school years as teachers introduced him to new authors. John Steinbeck's *The Grapes of Wrath*, William Golding's *Lord of the Flies*, Henry G. Felsen's *Hot Rod*, Thomas Hardy's *Jude the Obscure*, and John D. MacDonald's *The End of Night* particularly captured his interest.

In high school, King's taste in literature grew to include non–science fiction writers like John Steinbeck.

Writing for School

Lisbon High offered King his first opportunities to write for publication. In his sophomore year he joined the staff of the school's newspaper, to which he frequently contributed articles. In his junior year he agreed to become the paper's editor.

Far more fun, and certainly more illustrative of King's personality, was a parody of the school newspaper that he wrote and published. Titled the *Village Vomit,* King employed his keen observation skills and biting humor to skewer all aspects of high-school life, from athletics and homecoming to the "in crowd" and the "out crowd." He often overstepped the boundaries of what the high school's principal defined as good taste, especially when he targeted various teachers. More than once the school administrator threatened to suspend King because of caustic remarks about a member of the faculty or staff; on one occasion he did suspend King for three days.

Fortunately, King's principal saw talent in his rebellious student and attempted to direct it constructively. He contacted John Gould, the editor of the local *Lisbon Enterprise* newspaper, who agreed to hire King as a reporter to cover area high-school sports. In return, King received five cents for each word published.

John Gould proved to be a positive influence on King. Gould emphasized that King could not simply write a story and move on; he had to revise the piece as often as needed until he had it perfected. King had previously relied on his raw talent to create his stories, but Gould succeeded in adding discipline to the young writer's routine. King later credited Gould with teaching him the fundamentals of sound writing.

King Enters the Publishing Fray

King and his friend Christopher Chesley passed many nights reading their favorite stories aloud to each other. In these sessions they encountered masters of horror, such as Richard Matheson and Shirley Jackson, whom they used as models for their own writing. The two friends also improvised stories in which King would write the first paragraph, Chesley the second paragraph, King the third, and so on.

A King-Chesley Production

According to George Beahm's *The Stephen King Story*, in 1963 King and Christopher Chesley collaborated on a collection of stories titled *People, Places, and Things—Volume I*. The pamphlet, copied on an old mimeograph machine so they could hand it out to friends, claimed that this was "a book for people who would enjoy being pleasantly thrilled for a few moments," but the budding authors warned readers in the foreword that "if you have no imagination, stop right here. This book is not for you." The teenagers hoped the reader would enjoy the stories, and they asserted that "the next time you lie in bed and hear an unreasonable creak or thump, you can try to explain it away. . . . But try Steve King's and Chris Chesley's explanation: *People, Places, and Things*."

The story titles selected by the sixteen-year-old King hint at what his future held in store. The pamphlet included such King stories as "I'm Falling," "I've Got to Get Away!" "Hotel at the End of the Road," "The Dimension Warp," and "The Thing at the Bottom of the Well."

Apart from his school-related writing, King spent hours in front of his ancient typewriter at home, putting his numerous ideas into words. Although King worked diligently at his writing, he quickly learned that hard work does not instantly result in success. At age twelve, King received the first of many rejection slips from a publisher. David King recalls that his brother was "constantly at the typewriter" and offered his work to various magazines, but he received "lots of rejection slips. If I remember correctly, there was a nail pounded in the wall up in the bedroom, and he'd spear all the rejection slips on it."[45]

The rejections hurt the young writer, but he tacked them to the wall as a reminder that he had to keep going and that if he trusted his talent, others would eventually recognize his skills as well. Chesley comments on the rejections: "In an odd way, they were trophies. They depressed him, but he knew that he was paying his dues."[46]

His First Acceptance

In 1965, after a series of magazines declined King's work, the horror magazine *Comics Review* accepted two of his stories. The first, "I Was a Teenage Grave Robber," tells the story of an orphaned teenager who retrieves corpses from the local cemetery so that a mad scientist can perform experiments on them. As the reader expects, the scientist unintentionally creates hideous monsters that grow from the maggots infesting the bodies, requiring the teenager to rescue the town and his girlfriend by destroying the monsters. A second story followed, which King titled "The Star Invaders." Though he received no payment for either story, the acceptances of his work gave King hope.

King also wrote his first novel during his high school years. Though never published, *The Aftermath* depicts life in the United States following an atomic explosion. In this early work, King employed a contemporary social issue—the fear and paranoia produced by the specter of atomic war—to emphasize his belief that the nation had succumbed to Cold War hysteria. King would go on to incorporate social issues into most of his future works.

In part, King wrote because he felt uncomfortable in the company of strangers. It was difficult for him to make friends or confide in old ones. According to King, he feared "not being able to interact, to get along and establish lines of communica-

King completed his first novel during his high school years. It was never published.

tion. It's the fear I had, the fear of not being able to make friends, the fear of being afraid and not being able to tell anyone you're afraid. . . . There's a constant fear that *I am alone.*"[47] Through his writing, King could achieve both goals—he could express his innermost thoughts and, with his readership, he would never be alone.

The theme of not belonging, of feeling the pain of those on the "outside," permeates much of King's writing, and that theme likely is based on his experiences at Lisbon High. King observed how the so-called popular students isolated those considered unpopular, and he wondered what effects that treatment had on the outsiders.

"I would observe what happened to people who were totally left out and picked on constantly," says King.

> One morning, you'd come in and there would be "Sally Delavera sucks" written across her locker . . . this constant barrage until finally the kid would drop out of school . . . because they just couldn't take it anymore. High school is the last chance, the last place where you're really allowed to use that totally naked, violent approach to people that you don't like.[48]

First Encouragement at College

King's mother had always encouraged her sons to go to college. Once David graduated from high school, he entered the University of Maine at Orono. Two years later Stephen was accepted at Drew University near New York City. However, the King family could not afford the tuition charged by Drew, so Stephen opted to join David at the University of Maine. In the fall of 1966, armed with financial assistance from a scholarship and eager to develop his writing ability, Stephen King enrolled in classes at the University of Maine's Orono campus.

Nothing in King's experience had prepared him for college life. For one thing, the university seemed big: When he glanced out the window toward the fields separating the various dormitory buildings, he spotted "more people playing football than there were in my home town."[49]

He was also unprepared for the difficulty of college work. Since he had easily passed high school writing and English courses, King believed he could get by with minimal effort in those areas. However, a failing grade on his first college composition handed him what he labeled a "rude awakening."[50] King's freshman English professor, Jim Bishop, saw potential and encouraged the young writer. Bishop remembers three ways in which King stood out: he wrote every day, he always carried a paperback novel in the back pocket of his shabby pants, and he had read books by more authors

Jim Bishop was King's freshman English instructor at the University of Maine.

than any other student in the class. As Bishop explains,

> Steve was a nice kid, a good student, but never had a lot of social confidence. Even then, though, he saw himself as a famous writer and thought he could make money at it. Steve was writing continuously, industriously, and diligently. He was amiable, resilient, and created his own world.[51]

Serious Efforts

After living in a college dormitory during his freshman year, King moved off campus. At first he lived in a two-apartment layout with nine other students. Later on, as a senior, King lived in what he described as a "scuzzy riverside cabin not far from the university."[52] Though he enjoyed the companionship of his roommates, King still kept to himself much of the time. George MacLeod, who roomed with King, later explained that "Steve read like his life depended on it. He was writing and reading all the time. Basically he was an insecure kid who hid in his books."[53]

King's confidence in his writing grew with each class he attended at the University of Maine. In the summer between his freshman and sophomore years, he started writing the book that would one day be published as *Rage*. The novel carried a familiar King theme—a high school student who is shunned as an outsider and achieves his revenge by holding his classmates hostage.

In the fall of 1967 King reached his first writing milestone when *Startling Mystery Stories* magazine purchased his story "The Glass Floor" for thirty-five dollars. The inconsequential size of the payment did not bother King—he was grateful that someone had thought enough of his work to offer money in return. Before he graduated, King sold a second story, "The Reaper's Image," to the same magazine. In 1968 the campus literary magazine, *Ubris*, published King's "Cain Rose Up." Based on an incident that occurred in Texas, the story was about a college student who begins shooting other students.

Burton Hatlen

In the fall of 1967 King registered for a course in American literature taught by Professor Burton Hatlen. One day King appeared at Hatlen's office with the manuscript for *The Long Walk*, a book he had written that depicted the ordeals faced by a group of boys who embarked on a walk south from northern Maine. In the story, eventually only one boy remained.

According to Hatlen, he headed home with the manuscript "and laid it on the dining room table. My ex-wife picked it up and started reading it and couldn't stop—that was also my experience. The narrative grabbed you and carried you forward." Hatlen recalls that his student "had a fully developed sense of narrative and pace. It was there already. It was quite amazing to see that."[54]

Hatlen passed the book around to other members of the English department, who reacted in similar fashion. Though the writing contained flaws—one reader noted that King's technique of having the boys die one by one appeared too similar to other stories he had read—the professors admired King's talent.

Heartened by the favorable response from his professors, King submitted the book to a first-novel competition. A rejection letter ended his hopes, and a dejected King tossed the manuscript into a desk drawer.

Even at this early stage in his career, King's writing received criticisms that would be repeated through the coming years. Some of his readers believed that his reliance on horror should be no more than a passing phase—that gradually King should leave this format and enter what they considered "serious" writing. The university's president at the time, Winthrop C. Libby, recalls King's creative writing teacher, Ted Holmes, saying at the time "that while Steve certainly had a knack for storytelling, he wished that Steve would write more than horror stories."[55]

College Life

On February 20, 1969, King's column in the campus newspaper made its debut. He called the column "King's Garbage Truck" because its content was so unpredictable. Over the next fifteen months King reviewed movies, television shows, and music. In addition, he offered his opinions on current social issues.

Students at the university loved King's column because they never knew what to expect. In April 1969, for example, King called for a campuswide strike to protest the nation's involvement in the Vietnam War; in another column he supported the California grape pickers in their bitter strike to achieve decent wages. Typically playing the role of the outsider, King satirized campus organizations such as fraternities or the All-Maine Women club. King formed what he labeled the Nitty Gritty Up Tight Society for a Campus with More Cools, and in his column he dished out awards, called "Gritties," to anyone he deemed to have accomplished something cool.

Though his column fit his image as a rebel against authority, King refused to make statements just because other campus radicals were in favor of them. For example, although many college students of the late 1960s and early 1970s considered police officers to be the enemy and derisively called them "pigs," King criticized that point of view; he believed that the police deserved respect and support from the students.

While popular with other students around campus, King gave his editor trouble because of his habit of waiting until the paper's deadline to complete his column. As one staff member recalls, "We would be pulling our hair out at deadline. With five minutes or so to go, Steve would come in and sit down at the typewriter and produce two flawless pages of copy. He carries stories in his head the way most people carry change in their pockets."[56]

As a writer, King was prepared to do more than just criticize; if the occasion demanded it, he backed his words with action. When the English department conducted a meeting with faculty and students to discuss its curriculum, King criticized the department for not offering a course in which students would be exposed to popular writers such as Shirley Jackson. In an amazing display of self-confidence, King even offered to teach the class. Burton Hatlen remembers that King impressed everyone at the meeting with his arguments, and under faculty supervision King was permitted to teach a course titled "Popular Literature and Culture." Teaching, it seemed, would be part of his future.

Although he planned to become a writer, King knew that he would need a steady source of income, so he set out to earn a teacher's certificate. In his senior year King prepared to teach his first high school English class. As part of his work toward attaining a degree in education, King would spend the next few months as a student teacher at the Hampden Academy south of Bangor, Maine.

King's Gunslinger

While at the University of Maine, King tinkered with a story that years later would appear in book form. The tale, which combined a gunslinger from the Wild West with time travel, veered from King's normal subject matter, but he enjoyed placing two seemingly diverse elements into one story.

As Stephen J. Spignesi relates in his book *The Complete Stephen King Encyclopedia,* one weekend home from college King showed the piece, which he called "The Gunslinger," to his friend Christopher Chesley. "Now at this time, he was too poor to afford regular paper," recalled Chesley, "and so somehow he had 'inherited' some of this heavy yellow and green paper." After reading the first three pages Chesley turned to his friend and exclaimed, "My God, this is incredible!" As the years unfolded, Chesley pestered King to publish the story, which he eventually did as *The Dark Tower: The Gunslinger.*

A Bitter Time

At Hampden, King discovered that his political views were far less popular than they had been on the University of Maine campus. King had joined fellow students in antiwar demonstrations and mourned the loss of Martin Luther King Jr. and Robert Kennedy, both of whom had been assassinated. At Hampden, though, King learned that a sizable number of adults did not look with favor upon college students who let their hair grow long and advocated social reform or an end to the Vietnam War. When he arrived for his student teaching position, an administrator ordered him to get his hair cut.

King responded to the intolerance by writing about it in his column for the university newspaper. In the February 12, 1970, issue King asked his readers, "Can you imagine a country supposedly based on freedom of expression telling people that they

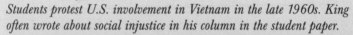

Students protest U.S. involvement in Vietnam in the late 1960s. King often wrote about social injustice in his column in the student paper.

can't grow hair on their head or their face? Since when have we descended to the point where we care more about what people look like than what they think like?"[57] King added a list of criminals who had short hair and wondered if everybody should look like them.

King's appearance also reflected the difficulty of his financial situation, for he was normally seen on campus wearing threadbare pants, torn sweaters, and dirty shoes. Tabitha Spruce, whom he met in the school library and whom he would marry shortly after graduation, explained the poverty her future husband experienced:

> Talk about going to college poor—this guy was going to college the way people did in the twenties and thirties. He had nothing to eat, he had no money, he had no clothes; it was just incredible that anybody was going to school under those circumstances, and even more incredible that he didn't care.[58]

Dave and Stephen's mother mailed them $5 each week for spending money, which was all she could afford. Stephen King learned later that she could barely manage to buy decent items for herself. "After she died, I found she had frequently gone without meals to send that money we'd so casually accepted. It was very unsettling."[59]

King frequently patronized a local coffeehouse where he enjoyed intelligent conversation and good music. Since the owner invited anyone to sing, King often brought his guitar, stood in front of the crowd, and performed country-and-western songs. A friend, Diane McPherson, recalls that King usually sang about the losers of life or those sagging under the burden of a horrendous streak of ill fortune. She adds, "I remember thinking at that time that Steve was singing about a version of himself that rang true."[60]

Graduation

During his senior year at the university, King's thoughts turned toward earning a living in the outside world he would soon face. Teachers like Hatlen and Bishop served as mentors, classroom and coffeehouse discussions sharpened his wit and expanded his point of view, and writing for the campus newspaper and other publications helped him refine his writing style. Now he had to prove what he could do with the talents he had worked to develop:

> During that spring [1970] semester, a sort of hush fell over my previously busy creative life—not a writer's block, but a sense that it was time to stop goofing around with a pick and shovel and get behind the controls of one big great God almighty steamshovel, a sense that it was time to try and dig something big out of the sand, even if the effort turned out to be an abysmal failure.[61]

King announced his graduation with an insert in his campus column. Relying heavily on humor, King called this his "date of birth into the real world" and claimed that his prospects were "hazy, although either nuclear annihilation or environmental strangulation seems to be a distinct possibility." He closed with the observation that "this boy has shown evidence of some talent, although at this point, it is impossible to tell if he is just a flash in the pan or if he has real possibilities."[62]

On June 5, 1970, King graduated with a bachelor's degree in English, a minor in speech, and a secondary-education teaching certificate. Armed with what he hoped would be sufficient credentials, King set out to land his first teaching job.

Chapter 3

"It's Enough to *Write*"

THOUGH HE WAS qualified to teach high school, in 1970, there were few teaching positions open. To make ends meet, King worked in a library, swept floors, pumped gas at a local station for $1.25 per hour, and collected $12.80 for an eight-hour day at a laundry. For the next four years King faced such dire financial straits that he did not know how he would pay his bills.

A Wife and a Job

Despite his poverty, King pursued another important goal. According to King, "The only important thing I ever did in my life for a conscious reason was to ask Tabitha Spruce . . . if she would marry me."[63] King and Spruce were married on January 2, 1971, shortly before her college graduation. Too poor to afford his own tuxedo, King waited at the altar in a borrowed suit and shoes. To add insult to injury, the laundry owner docked King's pay since he had missed a morning's work to wed Tabitha.

The newlyweds lived in a rented trailer in Hermon, Maine, not far from Bangor. While Tabitha completed her work for a bachelor's degree in history, Stephen shuttled from one job to the next while continuing to apply for teaching positions. In his spare moments, King worked on various stories that he intended to submit to magazines.

Tabitha graduated from the University of Maine in May 1971 and, like her husband, could not find a job in her field. In desperation she accepted a position as a waitress at Bangor's Dunkin' Donuts.

Finally, in the summer of 1971, the school where King had done his student teaching, Hampden Academy, offered him a full-time position. King leaped at the opportunity, though his position as teacher of literature and creative writing only paid sixty-four hundred dollars per year. Each night King returned to the cramped trailer, briefcase packed with papers to grade and books to read in preparation for his daily schedule of seven classes and one study hall.

He made an immediate impression on the students. As Brenda Wiley, one of King's students, recalls, the

Prior to finding fame and success as a writer, Stephen King eked out a living as a teacher in the early 1970s.

new teacher "told us that he liked to write, and I think he wanted us to write. He was fun and had a pretty good sense of humor."[64] The school yearbook emphasized King's penchant for a good laugh by including two photos of King. In one, he is reading *Mad* magazine; in the other he twists his face and arms in a menacing bogeyman pose.

King loved his two years at Hampden, though he rarely instructed the top students. As he mentioned,

You start off as a freshman teacher with a class you're least capable of handling. Which is to say you get the courses that nobody else who's got more seniority than you wants. So you end up with large blocks of kids who are majoring in smoking area and stuff like that. But I liked it.[65]

Financial Woes

King's meager teaching salary barely kept pace with the expense of supporting himself and Tabitha. The family's financial predicament worsened with the arrival of their first two children—daughter Naomi in 1971 and son Joseph the next year. Every penny disappeared into medical costs, food, and diapers for the children. Bills for the telephone or repairs to King's run-down 1965 Buick, had to be relegated to the "pay-when-we-can" pile. Consequently, King's car rarely received needed repairs, and the Kings constantly battled to scrape together enough money to pay one more monthly telephone bill.

To ease the financial crunch, King wrote stories for magazines, including *Cavalier, Gent, Penthouse,* and *Cosmopolitan.* Though these publications did not pay much, the money helped pay a few bills. When his nightly school preparation and grading of papers ended, King would retreat to a corner of the trailer to work on his own writing for two hours. While he enjoyed the creative give-and-take with high school students, he never doubted that writing would be his future. In spare moments at school King would barricade himself in the building's boiler room. There, squeezed into a student desk, he poured out his stories onto paper.

Christopher Chesley, who lived with King and his family at this time while he completed college, remembers that "more than once during the hard times before the sale of *Carrie,* a check for a story he had sold to a magazine came in the mail, money at just the right desperate time, enough to cover some bills and stave off the wolf a little longer." [66]

With mounting financial woes, King removed the telephone in an effort to reduce costs. He never knew when the Buick would run, and since school took up more of his time, he had less time for writing.

"There I was, unpublished, living in a trailer, with barely enough money to get by and an increasing sense of doubt in my abilities as a writer, and this kid was crying and bawling every night." In the nighttime quiet of his bed, doubts plagued him. "I began to have long talks with myself at night about whether or not I was chasing a fool's dream." [67]

Most of the time King shoved aside the negative thoughts about his career choice. He faced a perplexing dilemma, however. He realized that if he intended to make a living as a writer, he would have to sell full-length novels rather than short stories. During the stretches of time he would need to complete the novels, however, no money would arrive to supplement his teaching income. Could he survive on what Hampden paid until a publishing house accepted his first novel? What if he put months into a novel but no one offered to publish it? In the meantime his creditors would be hounding him for money.

Publishing Efforts

King completed his first novel, *Getting It On*, in 1971. The novel, which was begun before King entered college, tells the story of Charlie Dekker, an angry high school student who has been expelled for threatening a teacher. The student grabs a handgun, barges into his classroom, shoots the teacher, and holds the other students hostage while police surround the building. While authorities nervously wait outside, the students and Dekker discuss their fears, hopes, and failures and examine the roles of adults and youth in the current world. Finally, Dekker dies in a shootout.

King sent the novel to Doubleday, a company that had recently published *The Parallax View,* by Loren Singer, a novel that King felt was similar in style to his own. The manuscript reached editor Bill Thompson, who liked King's work, but thought it required revision. King was delighted that Thompson showed interest.

Success did not come easily for King. Publishers rejected his first three novels.

With rising hope, King mailed Thompson the revised novel. Thompson believed the book could be profitable, but he could not convince other officials at Doubleday that it would sell. When Thompson finally rejected the book, a dejected King faced the prospect of starting over on another book. King recalls the rejection as "a painful blow for me, because I had been allowed to entertain some hope for an extraordinarily long time, and had rewritten the book a third time, trying to bring it into line with what Doubleday's publishing board would accept."[68]

King felt that, in Thompson at least, he had somebody in his corner. According to King, Thompson "was the first person connected with the New York publishing establishment to read my earlier, unpublished work with sympathetic interest. He was that all-important first contact that new writers wait and wish for . . . and so seldom find."[69] King sent two more novels to Thompson, *Babylon Here* and *Sword of Darkness*, but he received rejections on both.

King later concluded that while his first two novels were barely acceptable, the third was "just terrible. After that I started to get it together."[70] King was polishing his technique so that one day he would be able to publish. King's first three novels served as his apprenticeship.

As David King says, "My brother paid his dues. His success was not handed to him on a silver platter by any means."[71] Each month spent "paying his dues" meant another month without money to meet financial obligations, however.

The Inspiration for *Carrie*

The jobs he had held before he began teaching, such as the one at the laundry, while difficult, offered King the opportunity to observe people. A female coworker at the time intrigued King. "There was a very strange woman working there with me. She was always quoting the Bible, and I thought, 'If she has children, I wonder what they're like.' That was when I got my idea for *Carrie*."[72]

He combined that thought with his habit of viewing events from the vantage point of those who are considered outsiders. Patterning the character of Carrie after two students—one that he taught at Hampden, and the other a female classmate he remembered from high school who was the target of frequent teasing and practical jokes—King began developing a story about an unpopular girl and her overzealous mother.

He wanted to craft a book that explored the outsider-in-school theme because he believed that "high school is a place of almost bottomless conservatism and bigotry." [73] By endowing his main character, Carrie White, with the mental power to move or ignite objects, he was warning his readers not to "mess around with people. You never know who you may be tangling with." [74]

After finishing the book's first four pages, though, King "thought it stank and threw it in the rubbish." Fortunately, when Tabitha arrived home later that day, she discovered the discarded work, read the material, and wrote her husband a note asking, "Please keep going—it's good." [75] Since he knew Tabitha did not lightly hand out praise, he decided to keep working on the novel.

Carrie Arrives

In January 1973 King sent the completed *Carrie* to Thompson. The editor liked what he read but felt the novel required further revision. King reworked the book and sent it in for Thompson's appraisal. The delighted editor asked King to meet him in New York.

The next month King, boasting a new pair of shoes and seventy-five dollars borrowed from Tabitha's grandmother, boarded a Greyhound bus bound for New York in order to meet Thompson for lunch. He arrived eight hours early, so he passed the time waiting in the bus terminal. Two hours before the meeting he started walking to Doubleday's offices, but before he had traveled many blocks his feet blistered from the stiff new shoes. King was so impressed with the city's skyscrapers that he almost constantly bent his neck back so he could look straight up. As a result, he arrived at his editor's office with aching feet and a stiff neck.

The two headed to an elegant restaurant, where King consumed two cocktails. Lack of sleep and an empty stomach, combined with the drinks, made him dizzy; when he ate the pasta he ordered, morsels stuck in his beard.

The day was not a complete disaster, however. Thompson explained that other editors at Doubleday had praised *Carrie* and that the prospects for publishing the novel appeared good. King returned to Maine and his classroom heartened by these words, even though Thompson warned him not to raise his hopes.

Good fortune smiled on the Kings, though, and in March 1973 Thompson sent a telegram stating that King's book had been accepted for publication. Trembling with emotion, Tabitha rushed to a neighbor's house to telephone her husband, who was teaching his literature class. When King answered, she read the message in an excited voice: "*CARRIE* OFFICIALLY A DOUBLEDAY BOOK. $2500 ADVANCE AGAINST ROYALTIES. CONGRATS KID—THE FUTURE LIES AHEAD."[76]

The teacher-turned-author hurried home after school to embrace his wife. Christopher Chesley stood by and watched as the touching scene unfolded:

> I had just gotten in the yard when Tabby [Tabitha] ran out the front door. Waving a telegram, she said, "Look, look at this!" I took it, and Tabby jumped and shouted, I jumped

Sissy Spacek in a scene from the movie adaptation of King's first successful novel, Carrie.

and shouted, and when Steve got home later that day, I got out of the way. They just hugged each other and cried. It was one of the best days that I have ever had.[77]

In much of life, timing is everything. Americans had in recent years been buying horror novels in large numbers. Ira Levin's *Rosemary's Baby* was published in 1967; four years later *The Exorcist,* by William Blatty, and Thomas Tryon's *The Other* made the best-seller's list. Publishers were hastening to fill the demand for such work just as King's first novel appeared. King believes that had he offered *Carrie* either six months before or six months after he did, he would still be teaching school.

"This One Is a Cooker"

With his twenty-five hundred dollar advance, King's financial pressures eased. He paid off debts, purchased a new car, moved his family out of the run-down trailer and into a modest apartment in Bangor, and reconnected the telephone. He now knew that he could meet his family's day-to-day expenses.

Meanwhile, Doubleday aggressively advertised *Carrie.* The company mailed memos to booksellers asserting,

> We feel it may be *the* novel of the year—a headlong narrative with the drive and relentless power of *The Exorcist,* with the high voltage shock of *Rosemary's Baby.* More than that, it is part of a rare breed in today's market—a good story. Don't start it unless the evening in front of you is free of appointments; this one is a cooker.[78]

An initial printing of thirty thousand hardcover copies arrived in bookstores by early April 1974 and met a mixed reaction. Customers purchased approximately one third of the books—a lukewarm response—and reviewers alternately praised and criticized the novel. The *School Library Journal* called *Carrie* "a terrifying treat for both horror and parapsychology fans," while the *Library Journal* castigated King's effort. "This first novel is a contender for the bloodiest book of the year" that will repulse many readers. The *Journal* continued that while some may enjoy the gruesome tale, it "cannot honestly be recommended." [79]

The novel gradually caught the reading public's fancy, though. North American Library issued 3.5 million paperback copies in 1975–1976, thus ensuring that King's book appeared in book racks throughout the nation.

King's success with *Carrie* could not be completely enjoyed, however. His mother passed away in December 1973 after a year-long battle with cancer. The woman who had nurtured his dreams and sacrificed so he could attend college did not live to see his success, although she at least knew that his book would be published.

With the money he received for the paperback release, King could afford to resign from his teaching position to devote full time to writing. Though he would miss the verbal exchanges with students and the discussions with hopeful young writers who sought his advice, King did not look back. As he explained in an interview, the money from *Carrie* "was a great feeling of liberation, because at last I was free to quit teaching and fulfill what I believe is my only function in life: to write books. Good, bad, or indifferent books, that's for others to decide; it's enough to *write*." [80]

The success of Carrie *allowed King to devote his full attention to writing.*

'Salem's Lot

King followed *Carrie* with an even larger success. As was true with his first book, the basic idea for *'Salem's Lot* came from personal experience. While teaching Bram Stoker's classic tale of horror *Dracula* at Hampden, King became fascinated with the problems vampires might face in the modern United States. He set the tale in a small town in Maine in which adults battle vampires for control of their village.

A first printing of twenty thousand hardcover copies arrived in bookstores—appropriately—near Halloween 1975. King's financial future seemed assured when Doubleday sold the paperback rights to North American Library for five hundred thousand dollars, half of which belonged to King.

Reviews for the second Stephen King novel mirrored the reaction to *Carrie*. Some critics praised King's storytelling talent while others contended that the author should have shortened the book, which was more than twice the length of *Carrie*'s 199 pages. *Best Sellers* claimed that *'Salem's Lot* was "a novel of such chilling beginnings that we look forward to losing sleep over it. . . . It is the kind of goose bump fiction that makes grown men afraid of the dark."[81]

On the other hand, *Publishers Weekly* criticized King, saying that he "elongated his story unnecessarily, so that when the same ghastly, gruesome fate keeps on overtaking the Maine villagers . . . one does begin to wish things had been tightened up a bit."[82]

In spite of the handful of negative reviews, *'Salem's Lot* achieved greater success with the public than King's previous ef-

The King Mansion

In 1980 King purchased a home in Bangor's Historic District. The twenty-three-room mansion, built shortly before the Civil War by a man named General Weber, reputedly was haunted by the late officer's ghost. According to local tradition, Weber died in the home but vowed to never leave the residence. The Kings, undaunted by the stories, remodeled the interior to include a study for King's work and an indoor swimming pool. A black iron fence bearing a bat-and-spider web design keeps curious fans from approaching too close.

Ironically, one of the few times King will not be found in his home is on Halloween. In his book *The Stephen King Story*, biographer George Beahm recorded that Halloween, which draws an immense throng of fans to King's neighborhood, has become a nuisance to him. When a reporter once asked him if he would enjoy Halloween at his mansion, King quickly retorted, "God, no! I'll be far away! I hate Halloween."

fort. When the paperback edition appeared a year later, 1 million copies were snapped up by avid readers.

Whether King was popular enough to place horror in the forefront of the publishing industry was yet to be determined. One indisputable fact existed: With the success of *'Salem's Lot,* King stood as a publishing phenomenon in his own right. *Carrie* and *'Salem's Lot,* however, were only the beginning.

Chapter 4

"Eyeglasses for the Mind"

T HE SUCCESS OF *Carrie* and *'Salem's Lot* created a market of readers eager to devour anything that King wrote, and he did not disappoint his fans. The prolific author poured out a steady stream of best-sellers that established him as America's foremost horror writer.

More Books from a Fertile Mind

In January 1977 Doubleday published King's third novel, *The Shining*. Set at the Overlook Hotel in the Rocky Mountains, the story unfolds as an evil presence traps visitors and fragments families. The book's strong sales—over 2 million hardcover and paperback copies combined—lifted it onto the *New York Times* best-seller list.

King's practice of drawing on personal experiences for his novels is clearly evident in *The Shining*. He and Tabitha had flown to the Stanley Hotel in Colorado for an escape weekend. Since they arrived one day before the hotel was due to close for the winter, the Kings were the only guests. As they roamed the halls, King wondered what might happen to lodgers who were threatened by a haunted hotel. *The Shining* quickly followed.

These three early successes led to a spectacular creative out-burst over the next six years. King wrote sixteen books between 1977 and 1983, including *Christine*, *Cycle of the Werewolf*, and *Pet Sematary*. He reveled in immersing the reader in physical and mental horrors, such as people who can read others' thoughts (*The Dead*

Jack Nicholson in a scene from the movie adaptation of The Shining. *The publication of* The Shining *marked the beginning of the most productive period of King's career.*

Zone), a 1958 Plymouth Fury that gradually takes command of its teenage driver (*Christine*), an influenza virus that devastates the United States (*The Stand*), and his most horrific novel, *Pet Sematary*, which centers on a Maine burial ground where the dead return to life. Labeled by *Publishers Weekly* as "the most frightening book Stephen King has ever written,"[83] *Pet Sematary* supposedly so terrified the author that when he completed the book he shoved it into his desk drawer for years before he could submit it to a publisher.

King conceived the basic premise for *Pet Sematary* on Thanksgiving Day 1978, when a car ran over and killed his daughter's cat, Smucky. The family buried the pet in a local burial ground used by neighborhood children for their pets and called Pet Sematary, after one of the children's spellings. King wondered what might occur if the pets came to life, then shifted that notion to one of humans returning from the grave. Besides dwelling on the typical horrors associated with death, in this book King examines what he believes is the most haunting nightmare for parents—the death of one's child.

Pets figured in another Stephen King best-seller from this same period. King based *Cujo*, a spine-tingling tale of a murderous dog, on two incidents. He read an article in a Maine newspaper about a Saint Bernard dog that attacked and killed a small boy. He also recalled the time when he took his motorcycle to a local garage for repairs; instead of encountering the owner, King came face-to-face with "the biggest Saint Bernard that I ever saw in my life. He started to walk across the road [toward me]. His head was down, his tail was down, he wasn't wagging his tail; and he knew what he wanted—he wanted *me*."[84]

Though the owner soon materialized and told King not to worry, the author imagined what might happen to someone in a similar situation when no one is present to stop such a dog.

Popularity Problems?

King's Doubleday editor worried that he might be labeled as only a horror writer and urged King to try other genres. King balked, telling Thompson, "I would write the things I had in me to write and leave it to the critics to figure out labels."[85] His intuition seems to have proved correct, as King has produced an enviable list of best-sellers.

By the late 1970s King learned that fame has negative aspects as well. Reporters and critics besieged him for interviews, publishers urged him to make book-signing appearances, and universities asked him to lecture. Hopeful authors flooded his office with so many written requests for assistance that King could not hope to answer them all, and numerous requests flowed in soliciting donations for any number of charitable causes. King wanted to help, but time and sheer volume precluded that possibility. As he explains, "On the one hand I want to accommodate people, on the other I need time for myself. Yet every time I say no, I hear them thinking, 'That stuck-up bigshot writer.'"[86]

While his family enjoyed the amazing chain of events, King cautiously eyed his success. For King, it was only a few short years ago that he could hardly pay his basic bills, and he feared returning to that condition. Tabitha urged him to enjoy the good times, but King kept a tight rein on his wallet. He had achieved success, but could he hold onto it?

"You Think I Want to Write This Stuff at Night?"

Stephen King supports his family in spectacular fashion by scaring the daylights out of millions of readers. Sometimes, one of the individuals he frightens is himself.

In one account of King's life, we learn that one scene in *The Shining* haunted King for six weeks. Paul Hendrickson of the *Washington Post* reports that King knew that he had to rewrite that portion of the novel.

> Six weeks away from the scene, he began to get the light sweats. Then it was down to four days, three days, two days. The scene, he says, is of an old lady, dead ten or fifteen years, lying bloated and horrible in a bathtub. She comes alive, rises from the tub, while a child claws at the door to get out.

When rewrite day arrived, a shaken King hurriedly inserted the alterations and put away the scene. Hendrickson asked King what time of day he typically wrote his scariest scenes, to which King replied, "Mornings, always mornings. You think I want to write this stuff at night?"

Themes He Explores

While Stephen King loves to scare his readers, he uses horror to entice them into dwelling on more serious messages. Most of his early books pitted children against monsters, but underneath the surface struggle rests a deeper clash. The monsters, though supernatural, can be thought of as symbolic of social evils that King targets. Educational systems that stifle individuality, parents who harm rather than protect their children, and adolescents who viciously turn on other adolescents receive heavy condemnation in King's books.

As he explains,

> I have no skill that improves the quality of life in a physical sense at all. The only thing I can do is say: "Look here, this is the way you didn't look at it before. It's just a cloud to you, but look at it, doesn't it look like an elephant?" . . . I'm like a person who makes eyeglasses for the mind.[87]

Time magazine, in a cover story about Stephen King, concluded that King's novels could be labeled "The Revenge of the Nerds" since he so frequently wrote about an unpopular student achieving revenge. Other themes that King examines include how childhood innocence is destroyed by the adult world, how youthful imagination dissipates as the adult world approaches, and how the government can be the instrument of death rather than safety. King loves placing "ordinary people in a pressure-cooker, in a crunch situation."[88]

Some critics prefer that King simply try to frighten his readers rather than educate them. For example, a reviewer for the *Washington Post* was not impressed with King's 1978 novel *The Stand* and suggested that King would have written a more compelling book if he had ignored the so-called deeper issues:

> King is best at dramatic action, a page-turning briskness, and this book is certainly crammed with the trappings of fright. If *The Stand* had paid more attention to arousing terror than examining the nature of evil, one might be willing to turn more of its many pages.[89]

King's Detractors

Throughout most of his career King has been a favorite target of critics who believe horror fiction is less worthy than other literary genres. He is frequently asked when he is going to write something serious.

As Robert Hunting, King's English drama professor at the University of Maine, says, "Steve and I are good friends but I don't really read much of him. I've read a couple of his books, but I like him better as a person than a writer. He's a very successful pop cult figure, and I'm a square. I have to remind myself though that Mozart also was a pop cult figure."[90]

Hunting's statement illustrates one of the biases that hound King—that he is not worth reading because he dwells in horror instead of "great literature." Numerous scholars dismiss King as inconsequential and refuse to read his novels. According to Michael R. Collings, a professor at Pepperdine University who has studied King's works,

[King] is enormously popular—and scholars hate that. He writes for a popular audience—and academicians hate that. He tells stories for the sake of stories—and theorists hate that. I have had colleagues introduce literature courses by noting that in that class, the students would read literature, "not that Stephen King stuff." I have had colleagues tell my students that they should never come into a university professor's office carrying a Stephen King novel.[91]

Carroll Terrell, another of King's former professors, defends the author, saying that he quit attending sessions of the Maine Literary Association because "they had such awful opinions of him. And these opinions were based on not having read anything of his at all."[92]

Other people criticize King for what they consider an overabundance of dashes, exclamation points, and other unique punctuation. As one commentator explains,

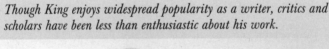

Though King enjoys widespread popularity as a writer, critics and scholars have been less than enthusiastic about his work.

memories and fantasies often find themselves pretentiously enclosed in parentheses. Sometimes non-punctuation or italics are used—quite arbitrarily—for gimmicky stream of consciousness effect. Occasionally we are subjected to all capital letters in parentheses with triple exclamation points (!!!ON BOTH MARGINS!!!)![93]

Even some of King's fans admit that he could shorten his novels without losing any impact. One reviewer has complained that King's style was "all *good* writing, it's all pertinent, but it goes on and on."[94] King should tighten his plots, they claim, and eliminate unnecessary chapters.

Not every reviewer condemns King, though. *Publishers Weekly* praises *Christine* because "it contains some of the best writing King has ever done; his teenage characters are superbly drawn and their dilemma is truly gripping."[95] More reviewers praise King than criticize him, but he still hears the complaints. "I hate bad reviews," he asserts. "That's standard. They hurt, that's the thing; they hurt."[96]

King concludes that he will never be considered one of the century's greatest writers for two reasons: "One is I'm not the greatest writer of the twentieth century." Second, he believes that when sales for a novelist reach the stratosphere, "literary" individuals assume he or she must have nothing important to say. "I hear it in the voices of people from the literary journals where somebody will start by saying, 'I don't read Stephen King,' and they are really saying, 'I don't lower myself.'"[97]

A Legion of Fans

One might wonder how King has managed to build such a loyal following. First of all, he understands that most people grow up with horror stories and like to be scared by something that cannot actually harm them. Even nursery rhymes prepare youngsters for monsters and mayhem. As King explains, "We start kids off on things like 'Hansel and Gretel,' which features child abandonment, kidnapping, attempted murder, forcible detention, cannibalism, and finally murder by cremation. And the kids love it."[98]

King possesses an uncanny knack for telling a riveting story. He loves to "put characters in a situation where the audience can't help them and where the audience will say, 'I wouldn't do that.'" He claims that he is similar to a tour guide into the mysterious: "I put my arm around your shoulder and take you around the corner and show you something that's the most gross awful thing you ever saw."[99]

King includes characters who face problems similar to those encountered by his readers, especially the problem of being shunned by society. In this manner King establishes a bond with the reader that carries over from one book to the next.

Readers also enjoy the humor King injects into frightening material. They purchase his books for a good scare, but they appreciate how King relieves the tension with humor. That feature of his writing comes from his own tongue-in-cheek views. For instance, he loves to joke that "people want to know why I do this, why I write such gross stuff. I like to tell them that I have the heart of a small boy—and I keep it in a jar on my desk."[100]

Although he is fond of infusing his work with humor, King takes his mission seriously. As he told the *Washington Post*, "The reader comes to you and says, 'Scare me.' When he picks up your book at the counter and it says 'CHILLING' across the

Pitfalls of Popularity

A bittersweet irony in achieving fame is that while it may bring comfort, security, and wealth, it also hands its recipient an equal dose of unease and caution. King learned this lesson almost immediately.

As related in *Feast of Fear: Conversations with Stephen King*, by Tim Underwood and Chuck Miller, at one book signing for *Firestarter*, an eager throng of fans surrounded the unguarded King. As the crowd inched closer around him, he "started to feel like an Edgar Allan Poe character, buried alive." Suddenly a woman screamed that she was being stepped on, and King wondered if he might be harmed. "The air was getting bad in this little pocket, as people in the back pressed forward."

The only way out, he determined, was to sign the books as quickly as possible and hope that the circle loosened. Gradually the number of people dwindled and allowed a shaken King to depart. From then on, security guards have become a common feature of King's appearances.

cover, what he says to himself, I think, is, 'Oh, yeah? Prove it.'" [101] As a result, King revels in taking the reader into places where "the walls have eyes and the trees have ears and something *really* unpleasant is trying to find its way out of the attic and downstairs, to where the people are." [102]

King believes he has triumphed if he is able to scare the daylights out of the reader. "You are not supposed to mess around and be delicate—*you're supposed to run them down.*" [103]

Perhaps the best part of King's horror is that it allows his readers to escape from their real worries. "People aren't really afraid of vampires, what they are afraid of is their own death . . . or the oil bill. When they are reading or watching my stories, they are not afraid of the oil bill, I'll tell you." [104]

Fellow horror writer Clive Barker understands that King's success hinges on his ability to make readers' skin crawl, and that in this he triumphs:

> He's selling death. He's selling tales of blood-drinkers,
> flesh-eaters, and the decay of the soul; of the destruction
> of sanity, community, and faith. In his fiction, even

Clive Barker, another popular horror writer, is an admirer of King's dark brand of fiction.

love's power to outwit the darkness is uncertain; the monsters will devour that too, given half a chance. Nor is innocence much of a defense. Children go to the grave as readily as the adult of the species, and those few resurrections that circumstances grant are not likely to be the glory promised from the pulpit.[105]

Although King makes his living as a writer, he appears to genuinely love his work. When King completes a particularly frightening portion of a book, he has been known to laugh in delight at what he has accomplished. He also is aware that this delight may seem a little strange. As he once said, "It's a very twisted sort of thing to want to do."[106] Legions of fans agree, however, that he accomplishes his mission.

Chapter 5

"Complex Characters and Great Dialogue"

KING EXPANDED HIS career in the 1980s in a variety of ways. He entered the decade with a new publisher since he had come to believe that Doubleday had neglected him. Even though King's books earned millions, Doubleday doled out miserly advances. Likewise, whenever King visited New York, company executives hardly took time to chat with him. His editor, Bill Thompson, was quoted in a magazine interview at the time as saying, "Every time he [King] came to the office, I'd have to introduce him all over again to the executives." [107]

Doubleday's policy of splitting paperback revenues fifty-fifty finally pushed King, who hoped to negotiate a more lucrative contract, to search for a new publisher. King eventually signed with an agent, Kirby McCauley, who closed a $2.5-million deal with New American Library, which agreed to publish *The Dead Zone*, *Firestarter*, and a third, yet to be completed, novel.

Enter Richard Bachman

The prolific King was producing two to three manuscripts each year, but his publisher hesitated to put so many new books by the same author on bookstore shelves simultaneously. Too many books, it feared, would saturate the market and stifle sales. King needed an outlet for his writing, so in 1977 he began publishing paperback books under the pseudonym Richard Bachman. Only King and a few executives at New American Library knew that he was writing under an assumed name. In 1977 New American Library published the first Bachman novel, *Rage*.

King maintained his secret until 1985, when critics and fans noticed similarities between Bachman's five novels and King's. In January a bookstore clerk in Washington, D.C., mailed King a copy of the copyright registration (a legal document that must bear the author's real name) for *Rage*. The next month reporter Joan Smith divulged King's secret in a story for the *Bangor Daily News*.

Though sales of Bachman books instantly boomed with the revelation, King was not pleased. He had enjoyed the anonymity of writing under another name, and he felt that the public had again taken over a small portion of his life. As he explained to an interviewer at the time, "It's like you can't have anything. You're not allowed to because you are a celebrity. What does it matter? Why should anyone care? It's like they can't wait to find stuff out, particularly if it's something you don't want people to know." [108]

In order to explore different themes, King began to write under the pseudonym Richard Bachman in the late 1970s.

In the 1980s, under his own name, King explored a new writing genre. For a long time it had bothered King that his daughter, Naomi, who was not interested in vampires or ghosts, had never read any of his books. He wanted to experience the excitement of watching his daughter pick up one of his books and lose a few hours among its pages.

Breaking the Mold

In response, King wrote *The Eyes of the Dragon*, a fantasy about dragons, kings, princes, and evil magicians. Released in 1984 by Philtrum Press, a small publishing company formed by King, the limited run of 1,250 copies was distributed to King fans through a lottery system.

More important to King was Naomi's reaction. The book, which he dedicated to her, depicts the struggle between the respected ruling family of the land of Delian—old King Roland, the beautiful Queen Sasha, Princes Peter and Thomas—and the sinister magician Flagg. Disdaining horror and violent material, King crafted a magical fairy tale replete with adventure and excitement, in which good triumphs over evil.

The tale engrossed his daughter, who read it in one sitting and told her father that she wished the story had not ended. As King recalled in a later interview, "That, my friends, is a writer's favorite song, I think." [109] Naomi's favorable judgment proved correct when, three years later, the book sold over a half million copies in the first year of its commercial run.

Also in 1984, King issued *The Talisman*, the only novel so far in which he has collaborated with another writer. Peter Straub had written *Ghost Story*, a book King loved, and the two decided that working together could be productive. King penned one chapter, faxed the material to Straub at his Connecticut home, then waited for Straub to write the next chapter and fax it back.

Fans of both writers, excited that two such renowned authors had joined forces, snatched up almost nine hundred thousand hardcover copies within two months, propelling the book to the number one position and keeping *The Talisman* on the best-seller list for twenty-eight weeks. However, the combination of horror and

A Ghost Story?

Has King ever seen a ghost? In George Beahm's *The Stephen King Companion*, King recalls experiencing an unusual phenomenon at a political fund-raising event in 1984. As he searched through a coat rack to retrieve his jacket, King spotted a balding, elderly man sitting in a chair across the room.

> I began to feel very strongly that this man thought I was looking through the coats to see what I could steal, and because I was feeling more and more uncomfortable, I finally said, "Gee, it sure is hard to find coats when people come in." And as soon as those words came out of my mouth, I realized that the chair was totally empty—nobody was sitting there. My reaction to this was to get our coats and say nothing whatsoever about it.

King and his wife drove to a restaurant, but before they arrived the stunning realization of what had occurred hit him. As King recalls, "I stopped and said to myself: *Now wait a minute, the guy was there—you saw him. Why are you pushing this away? You never took your eyes off him.*"

fantasy disappointed most readers who, rather than receiving a book in a style typical of King or Straub, found an unfamiliar blending of the two. *People* magazine's unfavorable review reflected the most common reaction when it stated, "In horror fiction, two heads are better than one only if they're on the same body."[110]

In the 1980s King experimented with another literary genre in a series of books featuring Roland of Gilead, a gunslinger whose training and actions resemble those of medieval knights. His goal is to locate the man who holds the secrets to Roland's objective, the Dark Tower. Titled *The Dark Tower: The Gunslinger* and set in the distant future at an unnamed place, the book unites two popular formats—science fiction and the western—interlaced with doses of adventure, time travel, mystery, fable, and fantasy. King announced in the book's afterword that more installments would appear. Knowing that he was working on unfamiliar ground, King apologized for delivering something different to his readers. He need not have worried, though. The book received an enthusiastic welcome. By the end of the 1990s, King had issued five volumes in the popular series.

By 1986 King had spent more than a decade scrutinizing the
same handful of themes—childhood terrors, the outsider, and
parents as threats to children rather than their protectors. With
the novel *It,* King brought closure to this early phase of his career. In the book's 1,138 pages, King resurrects characters from
previous books and allows them to destroy the monsters that
had terrorized their lives. Though some readers labored through
the lengthy volume, and even King promised that he would try
to avoid again producing such an elaborate work, he proudly asserted that *It* stood as a "final summing up of everything I've
tried to say in the last twelve years on the two central subjects of
my fiction: monsters and children."[111]

Into the 1990s

King next turned to a problem that had increasingly bothered
him as his popularity expanded. The more famous he became,
the less control he appeared to enjoy over his life, both cre-
atively and personally. King's fans, addicted to the books that he
so reliably produced, expected more of the same. But what if the
author hoped to pursue other arenas? When he attempted the
collaboration with Peter Straub, for instance, his fans complained that the book was not "true King."

More annoying, however, was the elimination of a personal
life. Fans clamored to speak to him, sent him thousands of letters, and besieged him with all sorts of requests. He had little
choice but to retreat to his home where, behind a protective
fence, he could retain his sanity.

As an example of the perils that fame brought, at one encounter with a fan King agreed to pose for a photograph. The
fan then pulled out what he called his "special pen" and asked
King to sign the Polaroid, telling King that he was his number
one fan. The man, named Mark Chapman, then departed with
his prizes. He later appeared on the front page of every major
newspaper in the United States when he shot and killed former
Beatle, John Lennon—after asking for his autograph.

Misery, which some critics have called his masterpiece, was
King's response to the invasion of his life. The main character in

King was once approached by Mark Chapman (pictured), the man who later killed John Lennon.

this thriller, Paul Sheldon, is a writer who created a series of romance novels featuring a character named Misery Chastain. Sheldon decides to kill Chastain in the series' final novel so he can write different stories. When Annie Wilkes, who describes herself as Sheldon's most ardent fan, rescues Sheldon from a storm and learns that he plans to end the Chastain novels, she terrorizes the injured author into rewriting the novel in such a way that Chastain does not die.

King did not intend the book as a criticism of his fans. He hoped readers would realize that his focus was more on an author being "labeled" by the public, in his case as a horror writer. King believed he had other novels to write and hoped he would get the chance to break, or at least expand, the bonds that restricted him to the horror genre.

In *Misery* King surpassed his previous efforts to frighten people. King recalls that one segment of *Misery* terrified him as he wrote it. In this particular scene, King has Wilkes chop off Sheldon's leg so he cannot leave her home.

The scene startled some fans. King received a letter from a woman who admitted that she fainted in a beauty parlor while reading the book. When an ambulance rushed her to a hospital, doctors at first thought she had suffered a seizure, but repeated testing showed nothing physically wrong. King explained that "two or three days later the doctor came in and said, 'I read the book that you were reading at the time, and my diagnosis is that you fainted out of fright.'" King, obviously amused at *Misery*'s impact, added, "I should frame that letter." [112]

In his 1993 novel *Dolores Claiborne,* King continued to extend his reach into genres besides horror. The book depicts the harsh life of a Maine woman—a character partly based on his mother—who survives by making tough choices and enduring whatever difficulties she encounters. The book explores issues such as spousal abuse and the manner in which modern society places restrictions on women. Happily for King, his fans loved not only *Dolores Claiborne* but also his other recent efforts.

At the Movies

King's work moved from the bookstores to the movie theaters in late 1976 with the release of the film version of *Carrie.* The first of King's novels to be adapted for film, *Carrie* enjoyed surprising success and helped the careers of many Hollywood figures.

The individual who most benefited, however, was the man who wrote the book—Stephen King. The hardcover version of *Carrie*—which did not even bear King's name on the front cover—had enjoyed modest sales but hardly made the author a celebrity. The movie's popularity brought increased attention to the author: The paperback edition of *Carrie* included on the cover King's name in large letters, and King's second novel—*'Salem's Lot*—sold at a brisk pace.

Though many of the film versions of his later works have disappointed King, he loved *Carrie.* He says the movie was "terrific" and praises director Brian De Palma because he "handled the material deftly and artistically, and got a fine performance out of Sissy Spacek. In many ways the film is far more stylish than my book." [113]

A Torrent of Awards

Though some "artistic purists" might claim that Stephen King has no place with literary greats such as F. Scott Fitzgerald or John Steinbeck, King has received numerous awards for his writing. He has helped bring the horror genre to the attention of the reading public and, along the way, has gently nudged readers to examine social issues more closely.

The honors parade began in 1975, when the *School Library Journal* added *Carrie* to its recommended-book list. The following year King received the first of his seven World Fantasy Award nominations for *'Salem's Lot*, and in 1979 the Balrog Awards handed *The Stand* second place in its best novel competition and *Night Shift* second place in the best collection category. Two organizations honored *The Shining* in 1978—both the World Science Fiction Society and the Science Fiction Writers of America nominated the book in their best-book contest. Four years later *Danse Macabre* received the World Science Fiction Society's Hugo Award as best book of the year.

Recognizing that King's impact can be beneficial to younger readers, the American Library Association included both *The Long Walk* (1979) and *Firestarter* (1981) to its list of best books of the year for young adults. In 1982 Great Britain also honored King by awarding *Cujo* a special British Fantasy Award for outstanding contribution to horror writing.

Since that first film, more than thirty Stephen King books or stories have appeared as major motion pictures or television miniseries. Between 1974 and 1983, six movies debuted to mixed reaction. Famed director Stanley Kubrick adapted *The Shining* in 1980 but so changed the story that King dismissed the movie. He claimed Kubrick "set out to make a horror movie with no apparent understanding of the genre."[114] On the other hand, King loved the 1983 movies *Cujo*, directed by Lewis Teague, and *The Dead Zone*, directed by David Cronenberg. He was dismayed, however, when he observed an audience viewing a third 1983 movie, *Christine*. "People just sat there. Nobody catcalled or laughed. And nobody was getting into it either."[115]

One problem movie directors encounter with King is that his writing style is very visual—the reader can easily picture in his mind what is occurring on the page. Directors experience difficulty trying to recreate the images on film, and when they fail, the audience responds negatively.

A scene from director Stanley Kubrick's successful adaptation of The Shining. *Not all of King's novels have translated to film as well.*

Another problem for filmmakers is that King produces lengthy novels. Since movies generally run about two hours, much of King's material has to be eliminated. This irritates his faithful readers.

King the Moviemaker

For much of his career King has remained out of the movie-making process. He recognizes that he can either become deeply involved in the making of a movie and accept either the praise or the blame, or simply sell the movie rights, and leave the details to the screenwriters and director. With the latter option, King advises, "You are in a no-lose situation, when you can say, 'If it's good, that's based on my work.' And if it's bad, you can say, 'I didn't have anything to do with that.'"[116]

King eventually expanded his involvement in movies based on his novels. In 1982 George Romero directed the film *Creepshow*. The movie included strong performances from such

Hollywood stars as Hal Holbrook, Ted Danson, E. G. Marshall, and Ed Harris; the film also featured Stephen King starring in the role of Jordy Verrill and King's son, Joe, as a little boy who owns a forbidden *Creepshow* comic book.

A delighted King proclaimed that he was "happy with *Creepshow* because I was involved with the entire thing from beginning to end." His acting reflected that delight and generated positive comments from others on the set. As producer Richard Rubinstein states, "Steve turned out to be much more than competent; he gave the role a life of its own."

Despite this experience, King has no desire to launch a full-time acting career. By filming's end, he complains, "I was in a chair for six hours a day getting this Astro-turf stuff put all over my body." He adds, "I didn't care for it that much."[117]

Four years later King, generally disappointed with most of Hollywood's efforts to adapt his work for film, finally agreed to direct the film version of one of his short stories. Reluctant at first to become deeply involved in a film, King finally succumbed to famed Hollywood producer-director Dino De Laurentis's persistence. As King explains, "For a long time I

Stephen King in his acting debut in George Romero's Creepshow.

thought maybe I ought to direct an adaptation of one of my stories, because so many people have said to me that the film didn't seem like the book." [118]

King the Director

Eager to learn if he could succeed where others had failed, King donned the director's cap for the movie *Maximum Overdrive*. Awed by the capabilities of modern machines, King created a movie in which lawn mowers attack humans, stereos explode in listeners' ears, and toy cars run down pet dogs.

Despite help from other directors, such as George Romero, King found he could not grasp the director's job. He worked such long hours shooting the movie in North Carolina that he was unable to focus on business back home. From July until October 1985, he awoke at 6:00 A.M., rode his motorcycle to a nearby McDonald's for breakfast, worked on the set all day, ate dinner at a small restaurant, then returned to his rented home to write for two hours.

In the four months it took him to make the movie, he could have completed a novel and earned millions of dollars in royalties; all he received for his directorial debut was seventy thousand dollars. King reflects on the experience with some humor: "I didn't care for it at all. I had to work. I wasn't used to working. I hadn't worked in 12 years." [119]

Reviews, even one appearing in King's hometown paper, found little to praise in the finished product. Within four months of its release, *Maximum Overdrive* had disappeared from theaters.

A much more successful movie crafted from a King short story appeared the next year when *Stand by Me*, directed by Rob Reiner, arrived in theaters. The story of four young boys dealing with the fears, anxieties, and doubts that plague most adolescents as they grow up showed viewers a different Stephen King. Although the tale includes a dead body, King's gentle examination of youngsters learning more about themselves is what most viewers remember about the film.

Reiner had loved King's short story and nervously awaited the author's reaction after viewing the film. The director recalls that after the screening, King

King (pictured with Emilio Estevez) made his directorial debut in 1985 with the film Maximum Overdrive.

appeared very, very moved and really couldn't even talk to us. He said, "I have to go away." And he went away for about fifteen minutes. Then, he came back and we sat around and talked about it and he told us how much of the story had been his life—and how upsetting it was to him. . . . He said it was upsetting to sit there and see all these kids he grew up with on screen, brought back to life when—well, you can't ever get them back.[120]

Having regained his composure, King stated that *Stand by Me* easily surpassed any previous attempt to bring his writing to the screen.

Stand by Me *was one of two Rob Reiner film adaptations of Stephen King material that garnered critical acclaim.*

An Oscar Winner

The most riveting King movie is *Misery* (1990), also directed by Rob Reiner. At first Reiner had little interest in directing the film, but once he read the script he was hooked by the notion of an author being trapped by his own success. He believed that he could construct a powerful motion picture, even though many other directors had failed with King's material:

> King is a good writer, he pens wonderfully complex characters and great dialogue. Yet when people adapt his books into movies they tend to . . . just concentrate on the Horror and the Supernatural—all the things that seem to be the most overtly commercial. It's a grave mistake because they lose many levels of his work by doing the obvious.[121]

Reiner's film received favorable reviews. King, delighted with Reiner's involvement, loved the movie. In March 1991

Kathy Bates, who portrayed Annie Wilkes in the movie, received an Oscar for best actress as a result of her performance.

The Shawshank Redemption, another film based on a Stephen King novella, earned actor Morgan Freeman a nomination for best actor. Though the Oscar did not go to Freeman, Hollywood's second recognition of a film based on King's work was gratifying. Interestingly, the works upon which these three films are based on are not true horror tales.

Other Stephen King novels have been adapted for television and have enjoyed success because, unlike a typical two-hour feature film, a television miniseries can last ten to twelve hours if necessary. This provides an opportunity to explore King's characters and plots in greater detail. During the 1990s seven King stories ran on network television, including *It* (1990), *The Tommyknockers* (1993), and King's own version of *The Shining* (1997).

Other Successes

In 1997 King parted company with his publisher, Viking/Penguin, and offered his newest novel, *Bag of Bones*, to the publisher who would meet or exceed his asking price of $17 million. Scribner Publishing submitted the winning bid; *Bag of Bones* arrived in the bookstores in fall of 1998. This newest effort features writer Mike Noonan attempting to return to his work following his wife's death.

King has apparently succeeded in distancing himself from horror. In her review of *Bag of Bones* in the *San Diego Union-Tribune*, Martha C. Lawrence led with, "For those of you who think that Stephen King writes only horror fiction, think again." Lawrence warns readers that the book

> *is* a scary book. Those who rely on King to raise the hair on the back of their necks won't be disappointed. Yet readers who hunger for deeper thrills will be satisfied as well, for *Bag of Bones* explores what its narrator calls "the sewer of our collective psyches"—that breeding ground of ugly realities like racism, greed and deadly revenge.[122]

By the 1990s King was firmly established as a writer of popular fiction. Refusing to take his own success seriously, King agreed to appear in an American Express television commercial. Beginning with the company's trademark, "Do you know me?" King continued his humorous pitch for the plastic card. "It's frightening how many novels of suspense I've written. But still, when I'm not recognized, it just kills me. So instead of saying, 'I wrote *Carrie*,' I carry the American Express card. Without it, isn't life a little scary?" [123]

As the decade draws to a close, King's success is assured. However, he continually faces new challenges.

Chapter 6

"I'd Just Like to Be Remembered"

Wꜱ Stephen King has enjoyed phenomenal success, in some ways he feels trapped by that success because other people's livelihoods depend on his ability to produce best-sellers. Were he to stop writing, he and his family would not suffer because he is financially secure, but he knows that others rely on him to continue turning out books. King labels himself "Bestsellasaurus Rex," a huge beast who is loved because he writes best-selling books. "I started out as a storyteller," he moans, "along the way I became an economic force."[124]

As a successful writer, King faces such quandaries almost daily. He enjoys prosperity and praise, but he also must meet certain responsibilities and challenges.

Responsibility to Work and to Family

King loves living in Maine, where he and Tabitha can enjoy a family life and an uncomplicated lifestyle. As he explains, "I guard against success, because you start to expect things, preferential treatment at hotels or concerts. I don't want that. I'm not any better than anyone else."[125]

Stephen and Tabitha have three children—a daughter, Naomi, and two sons, Joseph and Owen. The Kings have always done their best to maintain normalcy for the family, especially when the children were younger. In this effort they were not always successful. Owen called his father Daddy, until he left on a business trip; then Owen would claim that Daddy was heading out to be Stephen King.

71

Even ordinary daily activities incorporate elements of work, however. Each morning at home, King awakens early and goes for a four-mile walk. Along the way he reflects upon ideas for novels in a process he calls "sort of sniffing at this book in my mind."[126]

Following his walk, King heads for his home office, turns on hard rock music on the stereo, and writes nonstop for two hours. Unlike many authors, King writes his books without completing a formal outline first. Instead, he starts to type and simply lets the story take over. Though he formulates a general idea of where he is heading with each novel, he often has no precise idea what will happen as the plot develops. He explains that sometimes his characters assume control of the book and do things that surprise even him.

King writes every day, including Sundays, except for three days each year—Christmas, the Fourth of July, and his birthday. Whether he is at home or traveling, King makes time for his craft. He may write only two hours each day, but according to King, "I work seven days a week. I write six pages a day [1,500 words], and that's engraved in stone."[127] This pace enables King to complete an average of two novels each year.

To say that King spends two hours writing understates how much work he does each day. When he finishes his morning work, King heads to his business offices for an afternoon of answering fan mail, writing magazine articles and short stories, and

"Aren't You Stephen King?"

An incident involving the famous singer Bruce Springsteen illustrated King's impact on people. Since King has frequently mentioned Springsteen in his novels, the two decided to meet for dinner in a small New York tavern. As the two ate, King noticed that a teenage girl at a nearby table was staring at them, and he assumed she was interested in the rock musician. When the girl left her table and approached the two, Springsteen reached into his pocket and took out a pen for the inevitable autograph request. Instead, according to George Beahm in *The Stephen King Story*, the girl looked at King. "Aren't you Stephen King? I've read everything you ever wrote!" The stunned author, shocked that he would garner attention over his companion, provided the autograph.

kicking around ideas for future projects. When an idea is ready to be turned into a book, King begins work on it during the morning session, when his "serious" writing occurs.

Though most observers would disagree, King claims he is not prolific. "I just sort of write every day and keep it rolling. I think a lot of writers have a tendency to stand back awhile and sort of sniff around a project if it's not going well." [128] King, on the other hand, charges ahead and keeps writing.

When readers or critics suggest that King writes for the money, he quickly counters that while the money is nice, it is far from what motivates him. He writes because not writing is unthinkable. The money allows King to focus on his craft without worrying about bills and other obligations. "No, I was always writing this kind of stuff," he answers. "The money found *me*. I do it because I love it. It's what I do." [129]

King's lifestyle reflects an easy-going attitude. The six-foot-three-inch, two hundred-pound King normally dons jeans and a T-shirt or flannel shirt, and when Tabitha needs anything from the store, he goes. King admits, "If I forget [the needed item] and come back instead with an idea that I tell her will make us $2 million, she'll still say, 'Steve, I'm delighted, but we still need a loaf of bread.'" [130]

The Kings love living in Bangor because they share a kindred spirit with the town's residents. Since Stephen King speaks their language and knows how they think, he feels at ease. As King puts it, "I am a hick and this is where I feel at home." [131] When King leaves his house on some errand, his neighbors respect his privacy and do not hound him for autographs.

The portion of King's world that he has little control of is the presence of fans. Fans telephone him, write notes, stop him at conventions for autographs, and flood his office with requests for money or advice. King always knew that fame would bring challenges he had never faced, but the intensity of his fans leaves him both thankful and shaken.

"I love these people," King says. "I don't hate them. I get very few crazy letters. I do autographs because the fans support me and I owe a debt." However, King asserts that some fans step

Though his books have earned him millions of dollars, Stephen King does not live an extravagant lifestyle.

over the line with their demands and fail to realize that he needs some semblance of a family life. "It's a 50-50 trade-off. I want you to read my book; you want to read my book. We get off even. They don't have a right to my life, but they take pieces of it just the same. When I went to look for videotapes this afternoon, there were a bunch [of fans] outside my house." King sadly comments, "I've had a lot of my life amputated already." [132]

To protect his family, King has recently added security measures, such as a larger, heavier fence around his property. He enjoys freely walking Bangor's streets and chatting with the residents, but outside fans make this all but impossible. "I don't want to live like Michael Jackson or like Elvis did at Graceland. That's gross. It was bad enough when we had to put up a fence." [133]

Responsibility to Community

King's success enabled him to help institutions and individuals in need, especially his alma mater. The swimming and diving teams at the University of Maine have received donations from King. In addition, the author taught two creative writing and two literature courses at the university during the 1978–1979 school year when he served as the school's writer-in-residence. His fame has also helped draw more students to the university.

The Kings' charity extends elsewhere as well. They financed a Massachusetts arts and music center called Milton Academy, whose patrons returned the favor by naming their theater after King's mother. King comments, "As children, we need to have our dreams encouraged and nurtured. My mother did that for me."[134] In similar fashion, the Milton Academy hopes to assist other young people in developing an interest in the arts.

Naturally, Stephen King supports efforts to encourage children to read. When the Durham Elementary School's librarian wrote King in hopes of receiving a donation with which to buy much-needed books, King mailed a check for $10,000 and a note admonishing her to "Get 'em some great stories."[135]

An Unwelcome Fan

On April 18, 1991, the Kings experienced a frightening moment when a man named Eric Keene walked into King's office and demanded that King purchase a pair of contact lenses for him and provide him with an unlimited supply of cigarettes and beer. King's secretary turned Keene away, but two days later Tabitha heard glass breaking in the kitchen. She expected that her cat had done the damage, but when she entered the kitchen she spotted Keene.

As George Beahm relates in *The Stephen King Story*, Tabitha recalled, "I didn't have time to be scared. I was just shocked. My body was already making the decision for me. I was already headed toward the door before he told me he had a bomb."

Tabitha hurried to a neighbor's home to call the police. Authorities sealed off the street, then cautiously inched toward King's house. After searching for a few minutes, they located Keene huddled in the attic, clutching in his hands not a bomb but cardboard with calculator parts attached. Diagnosed as schizophrenic, Keene was found guilty of burglary.

King addresses an audience at the University of Maine in 1996. King has donated generous amounts of time and money to his alma mater.

Little League baseball has also benefited from King's generosity. In 1989 his son Owen played on the Bangor West Little League team, a collection of all-star youngsters from various Bangor, Maine, teams. Because the squad did not have enough money to purchase new uniforms for each player, the athletes wore the uniforms of the teams for which they had played throughout the season. However, the team had heart. After winning the District 3 Championship game, Bangor West beat every opponent on its successful rise to the Maine State Championship, which they captured that August. King, who loves baseball and had attended each game, wrote an article about the team for *New Yorker* magazine. With the money he received from the article, King purchased matching uniforms for each member.

In 1992 King donated $1 million so that the local Little League teams and adult softball leagues could compete on the best possible playing fields. Complete with grass infields, seating for fifteen hundred people, bright concession stands, and lighting for night games, the complex has been called by residents "The Field of Screams."

Responsibility to His Craft

Like most successful writers, King is inundated with questions from prospective writers asking how to succeed. His message is simple—writers must work hard and write because they love it. He urges authors not to "write your novel with bestseller lists or movie companies or rich paperback houses in mind. Don't in fact, even write it with publication in mind. Write it for yourself." [136]

King tells aspiring writers that they can succeed through discipline and hard work. He advises that if a person has been given a talent, he or she must take the talent and improve it through constant repetition. "If you write for an hour and a half a day for ten years, you're gonna turn into a good writer." [137]

In answer to those who claim that a gifted writer is born that way, King emphatically asserts that becoming a writer

> is a direct result of conscious will. Of course there has to be some talent involved, but talent is a dreadfully cheap commodity, cheaper than table salt. What separates the talented individual from the successful one is a lot of hard work and study; a constant process of honing. [138]

To that end, King urges young hopefuls to "Read a lot. Write a lot. But . . . if you want to be a pro writer, you have to write a lot." [139]

King has built a reputation scaring readers, but he opposes one frightening notion—the censorship of books. Most of his novels have been banned at some point somewhere in the nation, usually by school officials who fear the books' impact on "gullible" teenagers or by parent groups who believe King's books are in bad taste. *Carrie, 'Salem's Lot, Misery,* and *The Shining* are just a few of his titles to be pulled from shelves.

King calls censorship "a scary idea, especially in a society which has been built on the ideas of free choice and free

King's Hobbies

As mentioned in *The Stephen King Story*, by George Beahm, a lifelong interest in music motivated King to return to his guitar and join a rock group called the Rock Bottom Remainders. Consisting of other noted writers such as Amy Tan (vocals), Dave Barry (guitar), Matt Groening (chorus), and Mitch Albom (piano), the musicians perform to the motto, This Band Plays Music as Well as Metallica Writes Novels. Not as bad at music as their motto might suggest, the writers enjoy performing at various conventions they attend together.

King's most avid hobby, though, has always been baseball. He follows his beloved Boston Red Sox through every season and admits that he hates it when the World Series ends. After the World Series, King grows a beard that he promises will only be shaved with the arrival of baseball's spring training the following year.

Stephen King jams with guitarist Al Kooper (left) and band mate Dave Barry (center).

thought." [140] He has frequently spoken against censorship at conventions and student assemblies. During one September 1986 address to high school students in Virginia, King exhorted the young adults:

> I would just say to you as students who are supposed to be learning, that as soon as that book is gone from the library, do not walk—*run to your nearest public library or*

bookseller and find out what your elders don't want you to know, because that's what you need *to know!*[141]

Future Projects

Though King has been writing for over two decades, he has no intention of slowing down. In fact, a glance at his schedule indicates that, if anything, he will equal or surpass previous efforts.

He has exhausted earlier themes, such as children versus monsters, and has discontinued placing his stories in the fictional Maine town of Castle Rock, but he has numerous other ideas that interest him. He plans to complete more installments in his *Dark Tower* series of novels, which feature Roland of Gilead. Other possibilities include a book centering on baseball, a novel about an evangelist, and a novel concerning Jesus, although all of these are in the very early stages of development. He has not ruled out the possibility of writing more horror novels, especially since he has already written sequels to a few of them. He hopes to continue expanding his scope, however.

One of King's goals is to eradicate the stigma that most horror writers battle—that their genre is inferior to other types of literature. Like any professional, King yearns to be respected for what he does: "I'd like to win the National Book Award, the Pulitzer Prize, the Nobel Prize; I'd like to have someone write a *New York Times Book Review* piece that says, 'Hey, wait a minute, guys, we made a mistake—this guy is one of the greatest writers of the twentieth century.'"[142]

He recognizes that such lofty praise is not likely to occur for some time, if ever. He would be content, though, with a simpler thought. When one reporter asked King how he would like to be remembered, he answered, "I'd just like to be remembered. 'Cause I got a piece about some writer whose name I think was Joseph Hergesheimer or something like that, who was a big bestseller around the beginning of the 20th century. And I'd never heard of him. Nobody's ever heard of him."[143]

Stephen King intends to see to it that late in the twenty-first century the public will still remember his books—and shiver.

Notes

Introduction: "His Genius Is to Make Horror Acceptable"

1. Quoted in George Beahm, *The Stephen King Story*. Kansas City, MO: Andrews and McMeel, 1992, p. 201.
2. Quoted in George Beahm, ed., *The Stephen King Companion*. Rev. ed. Kansas City, MO: Andrews and McMeel, 1995, p. 3.
3. Quoted in Charles Moritz, ed., *Current Biography Yearbook, 1981*. New York: H. W. Wilson, 1982, p. 253.
4. Quoted in Terrie M. Rooney, ed., *Newsmakers: The People Behind Today's Headlines, 1998*. Detroit: Gale Research, 1998, p. 74.
5. Quoted in Ann Evory, ed., *Contemporary Authors*, vol. 1. Detroit: Gale Research, 1981, p. 335.
6. Quoted in Sharon A. Russell, *Stephen King: A Critical Companion*. Westport, CT: Greenwood Press, 1996, p. 12.
7. Quoted in Russell, *Stephen King*, p. 12.
8. Quoted in Evory, *Contemporary Authors*, p. 334.
9. Quoted in Stephen J. Spignesi, *The Complete Stephen King Encyclopedia*. Chicago: Contemporary Books, 1991, p. 20.

Chapter 1: "If It Was Junk, It Was *Magic* Junk"

10. Stephen King, *Danse Macabre*. New York: Everest House, 1981, p. 98.
11. King, *Danse Macabre*, p. 99.
12. King, *Danse Macabre*, p. 99.
13. King, *Danse Macabre*, p. 100.
14. Quoted in Spignesi, *The Complete Stephen King Encyclopedia*, p. 33.
15. King, *Danse Macabre*, p. 99.
16. Quoted in Rooney, *Newsmakers*, p. 71.
17. Quoted in Beahm, *The Stephen King Story*, p. 19.

18. King, *Danse Macabre*, p. 99.
19. Quoted in Beahm, *The Stephen King Story*, p. 19.
20. Quoted in Laurie Lanzen Harris, ed., *Biography Today*. Detroit: Omnigraphics, 1996, pp. 97–98.
21. Quoted in Beahm, *The Stephen King Story*, p. 16.
22. Quoted in Beahm, *The Stephen King Story*, p. 17.
23. Quoted in Beahm, *The Stephen King Story*, p. 17.
24. King, *Danse Macabre*, pp. 120–21.
25. Quoted in Tim Underwood and Chuck Miller, eds., *Feast of Fear: Conversations with Stephen King.* New York: Carroll & Graf, 1989, p. 7.
26. King, *Danse Macabre*, p. 104.
27. Quoted in Underwood and Miller, *Feast of Fear*, p. 25.
28. Quoted in Underwood and Miller, *Feast of Fear*, p. 90.
29. Quoted in Evory, *Contemporary Authors*, p. 334.
30. Quoted in Beahm, *The Stephen King Story*, p. 20.
31. Quoted in Harris, *Biography Today*, p. 95.
32. Quoted in Beahm, *The Stephen King Story*, p. 20.
33. Quoted in Beahm, *The Stephen King Story*, p. 24.
34. Quoted in Beahm, *The Stephen King Story*, pp. 101–102.
35. Quoted in Spignesi, *The Complete Stephen King Encyclopedia*, pp. 58–59.
36. King, *Danse Macabre*, p. 100.
37. Quoted in Beahm, *The Stephen King Story*, pp. 22–23.
38. King, *Danse Macabre*, p. 102.
39. Quoted in Spignesi, *The Complete Stephen King Encyclopedia*, p. 32.
40. Quoted in Beahm, *The Stephen King Story*, p. 21.
41. Quoted in Beahm, *The Stephen King Story*, p. 23.
42. Quoted in Beahm, *The Stephen King Story*, p. 23.

Chapter 2: "This Boy Has Shown Evidence of Some Talent"

43. Quoted in Beahm, *The Stephen King Story*, p. 35.
44. Quoted in Underwood and Miller, *Feast of Fear*, p. 90.
45. Quoted in Spignesi, *The Complete Stephen King Encyclopedia*, p. 10.
46. Quoted in Beahm, *The Stephen King Story*, p. 27.
47. Quoted in Chuck Miller and Tim Underwood, eds., *Bare*

Bones: Conversations on Terror with Stephen King. New York: Warner Books, 1989, p. 90.

48. Quoted in Beahm, *The Stephen King Story*, p. 30.
49. Quoted in Beahm, *The Stephen King Story*, p. 37.
50. Quoted in Underwood and Miller, *Feast of Fear*, p. 250.
51. Quoted in Beahm, *The Stephen King Story*, p. 38.
52. Quoted in Beahm, *The Stephen King Companion*, p. 24.
53. Quoted in Beahm, *The Stephen King Companion*, p. 24.
54. Quoted in Beahm, *The Stephen King Story*, p. 39.
55. Quoted in Beahm, *The Stephen King Companion*, p. 24.
56. Quoted in Underwood and Miller, *Feast of Fear*, p. 2.
57. Quoted in Beahm, *The Stephen King Story*, p. 46.
58. Quoted in Douglas E. Winter, *Stephen King: The Art of Darkness.* New York: New American Library, 1984, p. 26.
59. Quoted in Harris, *Biography Today*, p. 96.
60. Quoted in Beahm, *The Stephen King Companion*, p. 23.
61. Quoted in Beahm, *The Stephen King Companion*, pp. 25–26.
62. Quoted in Beahm, *The Stephen King Companion*, p. 20.

Chapter 3: "It's Enough to *Write*"

63. Quoted in Rooney, *Newsmakers*, p. 71.
64. Quoted in Beahm, *The Stephen King Story*, p. 56.
65. Quoted in Underwood and Miller, *Feast of Fear*, p. 250.
66. Quoted in Beahm, *The Stephen King Story*, p. 12.
67. Quoted in Beahm, *The Stephen King Story*, pp. 56, 58.
68. Quoted in Beahm, *The Stephen King Story*, p. 56.
69. King, *Danse Macabre*, p. 9.
70. Quoted in Underwood and Miller, *Feast of Fear*, p. 33.
71. Quoted in Spignesi, *The Complete Stephen King Encyclopedia*, p. 35.
72. Quoted in Evory, *Contemporary Authors*, p. 334.
73. Quoted in Moritz, *Current Biography Yearbook, 1981*, p. 254.
74. Quoted in Evory, *Contemporary Authors*, p. 334.
75. Quoted in Harris, *Biography Today*, p. 97.
76. Quoted in Harris, *Biography Today*, pp. 97–98.
77. Quoted in Beahm, *The Stephen King Story*, p. 62.
78. Quoted in Beahm, *The Stephen King Story*, p. 65.
79. Quoted in Beahm, *The Stephen King Story*, p. 66.
80. Quoted in Beahm, *The Stephen King Story*, p. 64.

81. Quoted in Evory, *Contemporary Authors*, p. 334.
82. Quoted in Evory, *Contemporary Authors*, p. 334.

Chapter 4: "Eyeglasses for the Mind"

83. Quoted in Beahm, *The Stephen King Companion*, p. 242.
84. Quoted in Beahm, *The Stephen King Story*, p. 81.
85. Quoted in Beahm, *The Stephen King Story*, p. 64.
86. Quoted in Beahm, *The Stephen King Story*, p. 75.
87. Quoted in Underwood and Miller, *Feast of Fear*, p. 38.
88. Quoted in Underwood and Miller, *Feast of Fear*, p. 64.
89. Quoted in Evory, *Contemporary Authors*, p. 335.
90. Quoted in Beahm, *The Stephen King Companion*, p. 26.
91. Quoted in Beahm, *The Stephen King Companion*, pp. 187–88.
92. Quoted in Beahm, *The Stephen King Companion*, p. 27.
93. Quoted in Evory, *Contemporary Authors*, p. 334.
94. Quoted in Evory, *Contemporary Authors*, p. 335.
95. Quoted in Beahm, *The Stephen King Story*, p. 109.
96. Quoted in Underwood and Miller, *Feast of Fear*, p. 16.
97. Quoted in Beahm, *The Stephen King Companion*, pp. 78–79.
98. Quoted in Rooney, *Newsmakers*, p. 72.
99. Quoted in Underwood and Miller, *Feast of Fear*, p. 246.
100. Quoted in Rooney, *Newsmakers*, p. 71.
101. Quoted in Evory, *Contemporary Authors*, p. 335.
102. Quoted in Spignesi, *The Complete Stephen King Encyclopedia*, p. 10.
103. Quoted in Beahm, *The Stephen King Companion*, p. 51.
104. Quoted in Underwood and Miller, *Feast of Fear*, p. 6.
105. Quoted in Beahm, *The Stephen King Companion*, p. 3.
106. Quoted in Underwood and Miller, *Feast of Fear*, p. 246.

Chapter 5: "Complex Characters and Great Dialogue"

107. Quoted in Beahm, *The Stephen King Story*, pp. 78–79.
108. Quoted in Beahm, *The Stephen King Story*, p. 122.
109. Quoted in Beahm, *The Stephen King Story*, p. 137.
110. Quoted in Beahm, *The Stephen King Companion*, p. 248.
111. Quoted in Beahm, *The Stephen King Companion*, p. 263.
112. Quoted in Underwood and Miller, *Feast of Fear*, p. 266.
113. Quoted in Ann Lloyd, *The Films of Stephen King*. New York: St. Martin's Press, 1993, p. 15.

114. Quoted in Lloyd, *The Films of Stephen King*, p. 19.
115. Quoted in Lloyd, *The Films of Stephen King*, p. 34.
116. Quoted in Beahm, *The Stephen King Story*, p. 88.
117. Quoted in Lloyd, *The Films of Stephen King*, pp. 22–23.
118. Quoted in Lloyd, *The Films of Stephen King*, p. 47.
119. Quoted in Beahm, *The Stephen King Story*, p. 127.
120. Quoted in Spignesi, *The Complete Stephen King Encyclopedia*, p. 49.
121. Quoted in Lloyd, *The Films of Stephen King*, p. 71.
122. Quoted in Martha C. Lawrence, "Inside These '*Bones*'," *San Diego Union-Tribune*, September 27, 1998, pp. 1–4.
123. Quoted in Beahm, *The Stephen King Story*, p. 105.

Chapter 6: "I'd Just Like to Be Remembered"
124. Quoted in Beahm, *The Stephen King Companion*, p. 29.
125. Quoted in Spignesi, *The Complete Stephen King Encyclopedia*, p. 22.
126. Quoted in Underwood and Miller, *Feast of Fear*, p. 218.
127. Quoted in Underwood and Miller, *Bare Bones*, p. 75.
128. Quoted in Underwood and Miller, *Feast of Fear*, p. 99.
129. Quoted in Underwood and Miller, *Feast of Fear*, p. 13.
130. Quoted in Anne Saidman, *Stephen King: Master of Horror*. Minneapolis: Lerner, 1992, p. 49.
131. Quoted in Underwood and Miller, *Feast of Fear*, p. 255.
132. Quoted in Beahm, *The Stephen King Story*, p. 117.
133. Quoted in Beahm, *The Stephen King Story*, p. 162.
134. Quoted in Beahm, *The Stephen King Story*, p. 146.
135. Quoted in Beahm, *The Stephen King Story*, p. 189.
136. Quoted in Harris, *Biography Today*, p. 100.
137. King, *Danse Macabre*, p. 97.
138. Quoted in Beahm, *The Stephen King Story*, p. 27.
139. Quoted in Underwood and Miller, *Feast of Fear*, p. 256.
140. Quoted in Beahm, *The Stephen King Story*, p. 187.
141. Quoted in Beahm, *The Stephen King Companion*, p. 49.
142. Quoted in Beahm, *The Stephen King Companion*, p. 78.
143. Quoted in Underwood and Miller, *Feast of Fear*, p. 249.

Important Dates in the Life of Stephen King

1947

Stephen Edwin King is born in Portland, Maine, on September 21.

1951

King listens to the radio adaptation of Ray Bradbury's "Mars Is Heaven!"

1954

King's mother reads him *Dr. Jekyll and Mr. Hyde.*

1959

King's brother, David, produces *Dave's Rag.*

1962

King graduates from his one-room schoolhouse; enters Lisbon High School.

1963

King and Christopher Chesley collaborate on *People, Places, and Things—Volume I.*

1965

Comics Review accepts "I Was a Teenage Grave Robber" and "The Star Invaders."

1966

King enters the University of Maine at Orono.

1967

King makes his first professional sale when *Startling Mystery Stories* publishes his story "The Glass Floor."

1969

King begins his campus column, "King's Garbage Truck."

1970

King graduates from the University of Maine.

1971

King marries Tabitha Spruce on January 2; he starts teaching at Hampden Academy; daughter Naomi is born.

1972

Son Joseph is born.

1973

Doubleday accepts King's first novel, *Carrie*; King's mother dies of cancer.

1974

Doubleday publishes *Carrie*.

1975

King's novel *'Salem's Lot* is published.

1976

The movie version of *Carrie* arrives in theaters.

1977

King's third book, *The Shining*, appears; he begins writing under the pseudonym Richard Bachman; son Owen is born.

1978

The Stand is published; King teaches at the University of Maine as writer-in-residence; *Night Shift* and *The Stand* are published.

1979

The Dead Zone and *The Long Walk* are published.

1980

King purchases his twenty-three-room mansion in Bangor; *Firestarter* is published; *The Shining* is released as a movie.

1981

Tabitha King's first novel, *Small World*, is published; *Danse Macabre*, King's only nonfiction work, and *Cujo* are published.

1982

The film *Creepshow*, with King playing a supporting role, appears; *The Dark Tower: The Gunslinger* and *The Running Man* are published; King receives the British Fantasy Award for *Cujo* and the Hugo Award for *Danse Macabre.*

1983

Christine, Pet Sematary, and *Cycle of the Werewolf* are published; movie versions of *Christine, The Dead Zone,* and *Cujo* appear.

1984

King collaborates with Peter Straub in producing *The Talisman.*

1985

Richard Bachman's identity is disclosed.

1986

It is published; *Maximum Overdrive,* the movie directed by King, is released; the movie *Stand by Me* is released.

1987

Misery, The Eyes of the Dragon, and *The Tommyknockers* are published.

1990

The movie version of *Misery* is released; *It* airs on television.

1994

The movie *The Shawshank Redemption,* based on a King story, is released.

1998

King's book *Bag of Bones* is published by Scribner Publishing.

For Further Reading

George Beahm, *The Stephen King Story*. Kansas City, MO: Andrews and McMeel, 1992. One of the most complete biographies of the horror writer, this book illuminates many facets of King's life and career.

——, ed., *The Stephen King Companion*. Rev. ed. Kansas City, MO: Andrews and McMeel, 1995. A fantastic collection of information about Stephen King that contains valuable information on his college years and summaries of his works.

Harold Bloom, ed., *Modern Critical Views: Stephen King*. Philadelphia: Chelsea House, 1998. A scholarly examination that focuses on the themes, imagery, and characterization in King's novels. Valuable for the serious student of King.

Ann Evory, ed., *Contemporary Authors*. Vol. 1. Detroit: Gale Research, 1981. A concise summary of King's books and movies that includes excellent critical reviews.

Laurie Lanzen Harris, ed., *Biography Today*. Detroit: Omnigraphics, 1996. An informative examination of current writers, including Stephen King.

Stephen King, *Danse Macabre*. New York: Everest House, 1981. A combination autobiography/critical evaluation of horror writing and films by Stephen King that provides a unique glimpse into his life and thoughts.

Charles Moritz, ed., *Current Biography Yearbook, 1981*. New York: H. W. Wilson, 1982. A brief summary of King's early career.

Terrie M. Rooney, ed., *Newsmakers: The People Behind Today's Headlines, 1998*. Detroit: Gale Research, 1998. A glimpse at Stephen King's life, influences, and work.

Sharon A. Russell, *Stephen King: A Critical Companion.* Westport, CT: Greenwood Press, 1996. A serious study of King's life and writings that focuses on King's themes, character development, and style.

Stephen J. Spignesi, *The Complete Stephen King Encyclopedia.* Chicago: Contemporary Books, 1991. One of the most thorough collections of material relating to and about King. The book includes numerous interviews with fellow horror writers and with associates of King.

Tim Underwood and Chuck Miller, eds., *Bare Bones: Conversations on Terror with Stephen King.* New York: Warner Books, 1989. A helpful compilation of information about Stephen King, based on interviews he conducted with the editors.

————, *Fear Itself: The Early Works of Stephen King.* San Francisco: Underwood-Miller, 1993. A valuable examination of King's first novels.

————, *Feast of Fear: Conversations with Stephen King.* New York: Carroll & Graf, 1989. Another compilation of interviews King has granted over the years that offers valuable insights into the writer's mind and the way he practices his craft.

Douglas E. Winter, *Stephen King: The Art of Darkness.* New York: New American Library, 1984. An examination of the horror genre by a scholar who has studied Stephen King's work in depth.

Additional Works Consulted

Neil Barron, ed., *Horror Literature: A Reader's Guide.* New York: Garland, 1990. An excellent source for information on the horror genre.

Ray B. Brown and Gary Hoppenstand, eds., *The Gothic World of Stephen King.* Bowling Green, OH: Bowling Green State University Popular Press, 1987. An academic analysis of King's writing by a collection of critics and scholars.

Jeff Connor, *Stephen King Goes to Hollywood.* New York: New American Library, 1987. An examination of the King novels that have been translated to film.

Jessie Horsting, *Stephen King at the Movies.* New York: Starlog Press, 1986. A readable summary of Hollywood's efforts to capture King novels on film.

Amy Keyishian and Marjorie Keyishian, *Stephen King.* New York: Chelsea House, 1996. A useful biography written for the teenage market.

Martha C. Lawrence, "Inside These '*Bones*'," *San Diego Union-Tribune,* September 27, 1998. A review of King's newest novel that contains insightful comments.

Ann Lloyd, *The Films of Stephen King.* New York: St. Martin's Press, 1993. A brief summary of the movies adapted from King's writings.

Anthony Magistrale, *Landscapes of Fear: Stephen King's American Gothic.* Bowling Green, OH: Bowling Green State University Popular Press, 1988. A critical survey of King's works and themes.

Joseph Reino, *Stephen King: The First Decade,* Carrie *to* Pet
    Sematary. Boston: G. K. Hall/Twayne, 1988. A useful sum-
    mary of King's early novels.

Anne Saidman, *Stephen King: Master of Horror.* Minneapolis:
    Lerner, 1992. A decent account of King's life for upper ele-
    mentary students.

Stephen J. Spignesi, *The Stephen King Quiz Book.* New York:
    Penguin Books, 1990. An enjoyable compilation of King
    data and trivia.

Index

Picture Credits

About the Author

John F. Wukovits is a junior high school teacher and writer from
Trenton, Michigan, who specializes in history and biography.
Besides biographies of Anne Frank and Martin Luther King Jr.
for Lucent Books, he has written biographies of the World War
II commander Admiral Clifton Sprague, Barry Sanders, Tim
Allen, Jack Nicklaus, Vince Lombardi, and Wyatt Earp. A grad-
uate of the University of Notre Dame, Wukovits is the father of
three daughters—Amy, Julie, and Karen.